THE AUSTRALIAN BARBECUE BIBLE

THE AUSTRALIAN BARBECUE BIBLE

Easy and modern recipes

DAVID COWIE

Contents

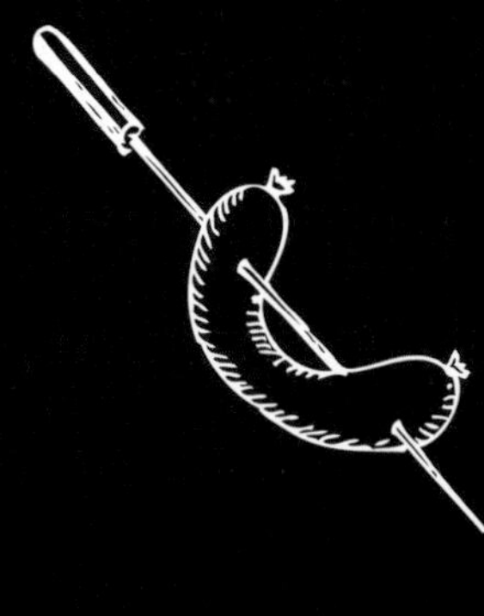

INTRODUCTION

Originating in the Caribbean as a 'sacred fire pit' for cooking whole animals, the barbecue has worked its way into the world's culinary imagination, becoming a cherished and highly evolved method of cooking. From the churrasco of Brazil to the braai of South Africa, the yakiniku of Japan to the good old Aussie barbie, the barbecue is an integral part of many cuisines. Considering the pros and cons of these differing cooking styles can often lead to long discussion, but underlying and uniting all opinions is one common factor: a love for barbecue. Indeed, while cooks may argue about technicalities, most people who enjoy a barbecue in one country will doubtless enjoy it in another.

What is it about barbecues that people love so much? Is it the wonderful smoky flavour imparted to the food? Is it the unmistakable brand of the grill bars? Is it the communal style of cooking where the cook is more often the centre of attention, rather than cloistered in the kitchen? It is all of these things and more.

It's eagerly awaiting the next cut of meat to be brought to your table at a rodízio in Rio. It's sharing a boerewors in the parking lot before a rugby game in Pretoria. It's a dozen people sitting under the sakura in springtime, everybody helping to cook thinly sliced yakiniku. It's relaxing on a hot summer's day, an esky full of beer and a barbie full of snags.

For many people, it's the timeless act of making and cooking over a fire. To some, cooking on a gas barbecue just doesn't seem right. How can food cooked over gas even begin to taste as good as that cooked over a wood fire? This may seem to be a legitimate objection, but it is primarily emotional and romantic. The truth of the matter is that exceptional food can be produced on either a gas or charcoal barbecue – you just have to learn how to produce the desired effects.

COOKING METHODS

With the advent of covered barbecues, a whole new world of barbecuing opened up, often allowing us to cook foods that we never would have attempted on a more traditional barbecue. Meats can now be slowly roasted over indirect heat so they become tender and stay moist during cooking. Whether you use direct or indirect heat depends on the type of food you are cooking and the look you wan to create.

VARIETY IS THE SPICE OF LIFE

When you combine your choice of cooking technique with our various spice rubs, sauces or marinades, the possibilities are endless. Add punch to basic recipes with a hot spice rub. Let marinades work wonders with your meat, tenderising the flesh

and charging it with extravagant flavours, whether you want a tangy honey and chilli combination. nutty satay, spicy tandoori or smooth red wine and garlic.

You can also use natural ingredients to embellish the smoky flavour from your barbecue.

Sprigs of fresh herbs, wood chips or citrus zest can all be soaked in either wine or water, then added to the coals just before you start to cook. You will not only scent the food, you will fill the cooking environment with wonderful aromas.

EQUIPMENT

The world of outdoor cooking has come a long way since the days of holding a few sausages over an open fire. Now, a few simple pieces of equipment will allow you to cook almost anything on the barbecue, while significant advances in barbecue design enable you to produce more exquisite meals than you ever thought possible. A drip pan and an instant-read thermometer, neither of which are very expensive, are essential for more sophisticated recipes. Your best bet is to purchase a disposable aluminium drip pan that can be discarded after use.

Often no extra equipment is needed – in most cases standard kitchenware can be used – but be aware that barbecue cooking can take its toll on tools not designed for this purpose. Although you do not have to purchase lots of equipment to enjoy barbecuing, you may find it beneficial to have some purpose-built items for your outdoor cooking.

Tongs are probably the most useful and versatile barbecue tool that you can buy. Use a pair that are at least 30 cm (12 in) long and spring-loaded. It's not a bad idea to have two pairs – one to move hot charcoal around and one to use with food.

Another very useful implement is a good, long spatula. The advantage of the long blade is that it will slide under any large food item completely, which makes it so much easier to turn over. Often, the spatula will come with a sharpened edge for slicing and prongs for piercing – these are also handy features.

A grill brush is a must for proper grill care. It is recommended that you brush the grill before oiling and after cooking, while the grill is still hot, to remove any food particles or burned-on grease. If you follow this procedure consistently, you won't have to wash the grill with cleanser, which ruins the seasoning.

Hinged wire baskets hold fish fillets, hamburger patties or bread between two grills secured by a latch. Simply place the food inside the basket and place over the heat. When one side is done, flip it over. You should lightly oil the basket before placing food inside.

Have all your barbecue tools ready and available before you light your fire. If using charcoal, always have extra available – there is nothing more frustrating than discovering that your fire is dying before dinner is ready and there is no more charcoal.

LET'S COOK!

Although traditionally the domain of carnivores, there's no need for vegetarians to feel left out at barbecue time. We have included a whole section on the fantastic combinations that only vegetables, fruits, cheeses and grains can make. Don't forget to serve these even if there are no vegetarians present – they round out the meal and are delicious in their own right.

A barbecue is a great way to spend a weekend afternoon or evening, or to celebrate a special event such as a birthday or public holiday. But don't only use your barbecue at these times – why not try cooking a regular weeknight dinner on the barbecue?

You'll fool yourself into thinking you're on holiday, create a tasty alternative to cooking in the kitchen, and there'll be less washing up!

Everyone loves a good barbecue, and with these recipes and simple tips at hand

HISTORY

Delving into the history books reveals that early explorers noted the way in which indigenous people would dry meat and fish on a frame fashioned from green saplings and placed over a smouldering fire.

Spaniards dubbed this makeshift grill barbacoa, while French settlers, who slowly roasted whole animals top to tail, coined the term, barbe-a-queue. The sophisticated variations that have resulted from this simple but brilliant technique have delighted generations. Fire, often a destructive force, has a creative power in cooking; its wispy by-product, smoke, adds a whole new dimension to the pleasures of the palate.

GETTING STARTED

This book has been designed to provide you with an overview of cooking on your barbecue and, where necessary, indepth descriptions of methods to help you achieve exact results.

Whether for a simple meal or a lavish affair, selecting the right equipment is essential; knowing how to use it to its maximum effectiveness is even more so. The choice of equipment can significantly alter cooking times, hands-on labour and, most importantly, the outcome of your food. For example, did you know that lava rock in gas grills is almost impossible to clean effectively and if it has a coating of burnt-on grease it can give food an unpleasant flavour? This sort of know-how can only come from experts in the field, and we are committed to passing it onto you.

From hardwoods to self-lighting briquettes, the equipment you use and the taste you are trying to achieve with your chosen method will influence your choice of fuel. To give you an idea of what is at stake, you will inevitably develop a bias towards hardwood chunks of hickory, alder, mesquite or applewood if you want to achieve an unmistakable smoky flavour in your cuisine.

Take old-fashioned techniques and apply them to a contemporary setting to get the best of both worlds – centuries-old traditions coupled with modern conveniences.

Whether you use the direct-heat or indirect-heat method depends on the type of food you are cooking and the look you want to create. To seal in natural juices, for example, opt for the direct-heat method, which sears your meat with a characteristic grilled appearance.

Combine your choice of cooking technique with dry spice rubs, sauces or marinades – taste combinations are endless.

You will be thrilled by what a marinade can do to your meat – tenderise its flesh and charge it with extravagant flavours. Whether a tangy honey and chilli combination or a smooth red wine and garlic marinade, you will find expert tips here on how to handle tougher cuts and how to prevent your marinated meats from being charred on the barbecue.

Whether using commercial preparations or homemade concoctions, there is enough variety in this book to adapt to family meals or special occasions. For the sake of precision, barbecuing is distinguished from grilling and smoking in that it imparts a distinct smoky flavour to food.

Experimenting with wonderful variations to all three methods of cooking, or even applying a novel seasoning to spice it up, has produced proud cooks throughout the world who boast that they have the finest fare.

EQUIPMENT

Listed here are basic grill shapes and types and other equipment you may find useful for barbecuing and grilling and, in some cases, for cooking over a campfire. Recipes in this book were tested and cooked perfectly on a four jet gas barbecue.

Other equipment, such as a drip pan and an instant-read thermometer (neither of which is very expensive), are essential for more sophisticated recipes. For simpler fare, little equipment is needed; in most cases standard kitchenware can be used, but use on and around the grill is hard on tools not designed for that use. Although you do not have to purchase a great deal of equipment to enjoy grilling, you may find it beneficial to have some of these items for your outdoor cooking.

There are many and varied barbecue models available today. It is very important to carefully read the manufacturer's instructions that come with each model.

KETTLE-SHAPED GRILLS

The kettle-shaped grill revolutionised outdoor cooking. The sophisticated design eliminated the need to control heat by lowering and raising the grill, and saved the cook from constant battles with flare-ups and uneven heat. The kettle-shaped grill is designed for cooking with the lid closed.

Carefully placed vents in the top and bottom provide adequate airflow to keep the fire going and completely eliminate flare-ups. Thus, searing over a very hot fire can easily be accomplished without burning the food. If the coals are moved to each side of the kettle and a drip pan positioned in the centre, food can also be cooked more slowly; this is the indirect-heat method of cooking.

There are two main drawbacks to the kettle-shaped grill. First, the lid is not hinged, which causes some inconvenience every time you open and close it. Second, the grill position is not adjustable; if the food is not quite ready but the fire is dying out, it's not possible to move the food closer to the coals to finish the job, which leaves you with two options neither of which is my satisfactory: finish under your kitchen griller or remove the food and rebuild the fire.

GAS GRILLS

The most recent step forward in the high-tech world of outdoor cooking is the introduction of a new generation of gas grills with sophisticated heat circulation and control. You'll find versions that have either lava rock or porcelain-coated metal bars. Both serve the same function – they evenly emanate heat from the gas burners below them and vapourise drippings from the food above, giving the food that distinct grilled flavour. In time, a difference between the two versions becomes evident. The lava rocks are nearly impossible to clean effectively; the layers of burnt grease give food an unpleasant flavour. The porcelain-coated bars are easily removed for cleaning and are dishwasher-safe.

Probably the greatest asset gas grills offer is the ability to control cooking temperatures.

Beefeater barbecues have units with two, three or four horizontal gas burners, that allow you to regulate the heat to the desired temperature. By experimenting a bit, you will find the gas grill to be just as accurate and responsive as your kitchen oven.

To some, cooking on a gas grill just doesn't seem like traditional outdoor cooking.

How can food cooked over a gas grill even begin to taste as good as food cooked over a mesquite grill laden with applewood chips? The truth of the matter is that a gas grill is as good as the person cooking on it. Memorable and exceptional food can be produced on a gas grill – food that is just as good or better than fare from a charcoal grill. You just have to learn how to use a gas

INDOOR GRILLS

Although this book was developed for cooking outdoors, most of the grilling recipes can be adapted for use on an indoor grill or if you don't have one, then on the stovetop or in the oven. The most current indoor grills can be incorporated into the stovetop or set up on kitchen benches, thereby providing a year-round grilling appliance. Both electric and gas models are available. Whatever style of indoor grill you choose be sure it is correctly installed and that proper ventilation is maintained. Check the manufacturer's instructions for recipe adaptation methods, especially regarding cooking with marinades and the use of oil to prepare the grill. Oil sprays are convenient for oiling indoor electric grills and cast iron griddle plates or pans. Do not use on outdoor barbecues. There is a danger of flare-ups and accidentally leaving the spray container on the side of the barbecue.

DRIP PAN

A drip pan is essential for the indirect-heat method of cooking. Your best bet is to purchase a disposable aluminium pan – up to 75 mm (3 in) deep rectangle – and dispose of it after each use.

GRILL BRUSH

This inexpensive tool is a must for proper grill care. Brush the grill before oiling, and after cooking while the grill is still hot to remove any food particles or burned-on grease. If you follow this procedure consistently, you won't have to wash the grill with cleanser, which ruins the seasoning.

HINGED WIRE BASKET

These baskets hold fish fillets, hamburger patties or bread between two grills secured by a latch. Simply place the food inside the basket and place the basket over the heat. When one side is done, flip it over. It is necessary to lightly oil the basket before placing food inside.

INSTANT-READ THERMOMETER

Old-style thermometers take too long to work to provide accurate cooking temperatures for grilled foods. The instant-read versions provide an accurate picture of the progress within 5 seconds of insertion.

ROAST RACKS

Made of aluminium or stainless steel, V-shaped roast racks do an excellent job holding large pieces of meat or poultry together as they cook. If you use one while cooking with indirect heat, you don't need to turn the meat at all; it cooks evenly on all sides.

SKEWERS

Metal and bamboo are common skewer materials. Metal skewers never burn up, but you do have to wash them. You need to soak bamboo skewers in water for 15–30 minutes before use to prevent them from burning. If you are fortunate enough to have rosemary growing nearby, try using these branches for skewers. Remove the leaves and soak the branches in water for 30 minutes. They imbue the skewered food with a pungent flavour.

SPATULA

Take the time to find an offset stainless steel spatula with a blade 12.5–15 cm (5–6 in) long – the kind professional chefs use. The advantage of the long blade is that it will slide under most chops and fish fillets completely which means they won't tear or stick when being flipped over. Stainless steel will never rust and is easy to care for.

PRAY BOTTLE

With the advent of kettles and gas grills, there aren't many fire flare-ups any more. But always keep a spray bottle filled with water next to your grill, just in case of an emergency.

TONGS

Tongs are probably the most useful and versatile grill tool that you can buy. Use a pair that is at least 30 cm (12 in) long and spring-loaded. It's not a bad idea to have two pairs, one to move hot charcoal around and one to use with food. (Of course, you can get by with one pair – you will just have to keep wiping it off every time you use it to move charcoal.)

FUELS

Shopping for fuel in a well-stocked market can be quite a confusing experience. Many different fuels now compete with traditional charcoal briquettes. Mesquite charcoal, hardwood charcoals, hardwood-flavoured charcoals, self-lighting briquettes and a number of different types of smoke-creating hardwood chips, chunks and sawdust all crowd the shelf. They all work well in the right situation. You must judge what will work best for you.

WOODS

Use oak, hickory, cherry, apple, mesquite or alder as a wood for outdoor cooking. Be aware, however, that, although a wood-burning barbecue is romantic, it doesn't make much sense. Wood takes a considerable time to burn down to useable coals and wood coals don't last as long as charcoal briquettes or hardwood charcoal. With wood you end up waiting twice as long to cook, and then your fire goes out sooner. Instead of using these woods as your major fuel source, use the smaller pieces as kindling and cut the remainder into 25 mm (1 in) chunks to add a smoky complement to your fire. Never use a softwood for smoking or as a fuel; the thick resins produce a distinctly unpleasant aftertaste. Be careful about burning scrap wood. Pressure-treated timber (the type of wood used in outdoor construction), for instance, contains chemicals that can be toxic.

APPLEWOOD

Applewood provides a subtle smoky flavour that is not nearly as pronounced as that of mesquite, oak or hickory. It imparts a slightly sweet but dense, smoky flavour, that is marvellous with poultry and ham.

HARDWOOD CHUNKS AND SAWDUST

Food cooked over hardwood has a distinctive smoky flavour. Hickory, alder, mesquite and applewood are the most popular and most widely available woods.

If you use a gas grill, hardwood chips work better than chunks. Select pieces 25 mm (1 in) thick and soak them in water for at least 30 minutes before you use them. Place an old aluminium pie pan over the gas heating elements toward the back corner of your grill before you turn it on, and place the water-soaked chips in the pan. As the grill heats up, the chips will begin to smoulder. If you cook with high heat, you may experience flare-ups from the chips so have your spray bottle ready.

The only limitation of this method is that the chips tend to burn quickly. You'll have to monitor their progress and replenish the chips as necessary, but don't put too many on at once or you will extinguish your fire.

For the gas grill, hardwood sawdust works as well or better than hardwood chips.

Easy to ignite, sawdust provides a consistent, flavourful smoke. To use, place sawdust in an old pie pan and place it directly on top of lava rocks or flavouriser bars. Turn the gas burners to high until the sawdust just blackens and begins to smoulder. Immediately turn off the burner underneath the pan. Replenish the sawdust as needed. Hardwood sawdust is available at timber yards, barbecue supplies stores and specialty cookware stores.

MESQUITE

Mesquite is a scrub hardwood tree that grows wild in the arid plains of the southwest America and Mexico and is available at barbecue supplies stores. Sweeter and more delicate than hickory, mesquite is a perfect complement to richly flavoured meats such as beef and lamb, as well as duck.

FRESH HERBS AND CITRUS RINDS

Thyme, bay leaves, rosemary, oregano and marjoram are particularly well suited to flavouring your fire. Chose one type of herb, moisten it with water (for an added taste treat, use wine or liquor to moisten it), and toss it onto the coals right before you put food on the grill. Try lemon, orange or lime rinds as well. Add them one at a time, with or without a complementary fresh herb. Be careful not to directly inhale the fumes of burning herbs or fruit rinds; they can be rather overpowering.

FIRE STARTING

Whatever method you use, allow about 30–45 minutes for your fire to start. The idea is to start the fire in your grill, not in your house. When you use a gas barbecue it will only take a few minutes to attain the correct temperature.

KINDLING

Starting a fire with kindling is probably the most individual and ritual-laden method. Each fire starter has a unique style, the basic method is to start with a few sheets of newspaper and crumple them loosely or twist them into logs. Place logs in the bottom of your grill, then place a handful of dry kindling on top. Place five or six briquettes on top of the kindling. Light the newspaper.

If the briquettes do not light, add more newspaper and kindling until they do. Once the briquettes are alight add more briquettes on top until you have a fire of the desired size. Everyone seems to have their own ratio of newspaper to kindling to briquettes. Just do what works for you.

ELECTRIC STARTER

Electricity is certainly the easiest and most foolproof means of starting a fire. Check the manufacturer's recommendations for starting a fire with an electric starter in your grill. In most cases, the instructions tell you to arrange your briquettes in a pile on top of the starter, plug it in and let it go to work. In about 10 minutes, your briquettes should be started. Don't leave your starter in any longer, or the heating element will be damaged by lengthy exposure to high heat. The only disadvantage to this fire-starting method is that you need to be near an electrical connection.

CHARCOAL CHIMNEY

The simplicity and ease of charcoal chimneys make them a wonder to watch. A charcoal chimney is nothing more than an open-ended, sheet-metal cylinder vented at the lower end, with a grate about 10 cm (4 in) from the bottom to set the charcoal briquettes on. To use, simply crumple several sheets of newspaper and place them under the grate. Fill the chimney with charcoal briquettes, and place in the bottom of the grill and light the paper. In about 10 minutes the briquettes will begin to smoulder.

Once all the briquettes are well ignited, pour them out of the chimney into the bottom of your grill.

A charcoal chimney is also the answer when you will be using your grill for several hours and don't want to replenish your fire with raw charcoal briquettes because of the fumes they emit when they just start to burn.

Simply set the chimney on an old pie pan on a concrete surface and light more charcoal. When the briquettes are ready, pour them onto your existing fire.

You can make your own charcoal chimney by cutting the top and bottom off a coffee or food can and making a vent in the bottom with a can opener. If you buy a ready-made chimney, you will find that it is inexpensive and has the added benefits of a wooden handle and a grate to set the charcoal on.

HOW MUCH FIRE?

When determining the size of your fire, first imagine the cooking surface that the food requires. Spread the briquettes out on a single layer to cover an area about 25 mm (1 in) past the edges that you have imagined. Now add about half again as much charcoal and you should have enough for an hour's worth of fire. Usually, 30–40 briquettes are sufficient to cook food for four people. If you are making a fire for slow cooking using the indirect-heat method, use about 25 briquettes on each side of the grill. Plan on adding 8–10 briquettes to each side for every hour of additional cooking time.

WHEN IS THE FIRE READY?

It usually takes between 30 and 45 minutes for a fire to be ready for cooking. Never cook over a fire until the briquettes are covered with a light ash and are no longer flaming. Cooking over a direct flame burns the outside of your food and leaves the inside raw. Your hand is probably the best judge of when a fire is ready.

Hold your hand flat over the fire at grill height. You will be able to hold your hand over a very hot fire for about 2 seconds. If the fire is hot, you can hold your hand above it for 3–4 seconds. If you can hold it any longer than that, you have let the fire die down too much.

Add more briquettes and let it build up again. A very hot fire is ideal for the direct-heat method of cooking; a medium to hot fire is desirable for the indirect-heat method. Once your fire is ready, carefully add hardwood chips or fresh herbs. Put the grill in place and let it heat up for 4–5 minutes before putting on food.

DIRECT-HEAT METHOD

Use the direct-heat cooking method to sear foods to seal in their natural juices and to give the characteristic grilled look. Foods that are low in fat, such as poultry and fish, and foods that don't take very long to cook are ideal choices for this method. Hamburgers, chops, vegetables, skewered items and fish fillets all fall within this category.

If using charcoal, start your fire and, after 30–45 minutes, when the coals have a light grey ash covering, spread them out one briquette deep so that you have an even cooking source.

DIRECT TWO ZONE HEATING METHOD

Preparing the barbecue for Two Zone Direct Heat gives greater control for cooking food. It creates a hot to very hot area for searing the food and a moderately hot area for cooking through to desired readiness. An outer third area may be created for keeping cooked food warm.

CHARCOAL BARBECUE

When coals are ready, pile two layers of coals to the left half of the area and one row to the right half. Put the grill rack in place and allow 4–5 minutes for the rack to heat. If you wish to have a third zone leave the outer right edge without coals.

GAS BARBECUE

Set the burners on the left side to high and the right side burners to medium to create 2 heat zones. To create a third zone leave the far right burner off.

INDIRECT-HEAT METHOD

The indirect-heat method of cooking is where recent advances in grill designs have yielded the most spectacular results. You can now cook foods on the grill that were unimaginable ten years ago. Whole prime ribs, turkeys and chickens will cook beautifully without even needing to be turned over. Foods traditionally braised slowly in the oven with plenty of cooking liquid, such as veal breasts and pheasant, can now be done outdoors.

If you are using a gas grill, pre-heat the grill with all three burners on high. The grill should be hot in about 10 minutes. Turn off the centre burner and carefully position the disposable aluminium drip pan over it.

PREPARING THE GRILL

Always arrange the fire so that there are areas of the grill with no fire under them. If some of your food is done sooner than others, move it to these cooler spots to keep finished food warm while the remainder of the meal cooks. Brush the grill lightly with oil right after you put it in place over the fire. To do this, moisten a paper towel with oil. Using tongs held in a fireproof mitt-clad hand, rub the oil from the towel onto the grill. This will help prevent food from sticking to the grill and will also keep the grill seasoned. Place your grill over the coals and let it heat up for 4–5 minutes.

If you are using pre-soaked hardwood chips or chunks or moistened fresh herbs, spread them out over the coals before placing food on the grill. The wood will immediately begin to smoulder. Now you're ready to cook. When using a kettle-shaped grill, keep the lid closed for the duration of cooking; regulate the heat by adjusting the upper and lower vents. The beauty of this system is the total lack of flare-ups, even though the food is cooking at a very high temperature and fat is dripping onto the coals. The fat vaporizes as it hits the coals, imparting a desirable smoky flavour to the food, but the fat doesn't have enough oxygen to ignite into an undesirable flame.

Heat circulation in the kettle-shaped grill is excellent, cooking the food on top as well as on the bottom. You still need to flip the food over due to the short cooking time, but it does cook faster and more evenly inside a kettle. So it is very important that the lid stays closed, except when you need to baste, add coals, check the food or turn it over. Otherwise, leave the grill alone and let it cook.

If you are using a gas grill, turn all three burners to high and close the lid. Your grill should be sufficiently hot to cook on in about 10 minutes. Depending on the food being cooked and the desired effect, you can leave the temperature on high while cooking or turn down one or more burners. There is a nearly immediate response to the burner temperature controls, so experiment to find the exact temperature you want.

Always keep the grill clean. The best method is to quickly brush the excess food off with a grill brush immediately after you finish cooking. This way the remaining fire will burn off any lingering bits and you won't have to resort to soap and water, which would ruin the seasoning of the grill surface. If you do not have a grill brush use a crumpled wad of aluminium foil held with tongs.

OUTDOOR COOKING METHODS

With covered grills, a whole new world of barbecuing opened up. Foods can now be slowly roasted over indirect heat so that they become tender and stay moist during cooking. Whether to use indirect-heat cooking or traditional grilling over direct heat depends on the type of food to be cooked and the result desired.

Put oiled grill in position and turn up the grill heat for 4–5 minutes. Place the food directly over the drip pan. Close the lid and let the food cook. Regulate the temperature by adjusting the two outer burners; leave the centre burner off. For recipes calling for a temperature of 180°–200°C (355°–390°F), turn the burners to medium. For recipes calling for 150°–160°C (300°–320°F) turn both burners to low.

If you want a smoky flavour, use hardwood chips in a gas grill. If you are using moistened fresh herbs, throw them directly onto the outside porcelain bars, then close the lid. Remember that these grills are designed to operate most effectively

when the lid is closed. Open the lid only to check on or to baste the food or to add more chips or herbs.

Another advantage of this method is the absence of the sometimes difficult-to-handle rotisserie. It simply isn't needed any more.

If you are using a charcoal grill, prepare your coals as per the Direct-Heat Method. When they are covered with a light grey ash, separate them into two piles on each side of the kettle. Place a disposable aluminium drip pan between the piles. If you are using pre-soaked hardwood chips or chunks or moistened fresh herbs, add them to the piles now. Put the grill in place and allow it to heat up for 4–5 minutes before positioning the food on the grill directly over the drip pan.

If you want to sear the food first, simply place the food directly over one side of the coals until it is browned, and then move it over the drip pan. Close the lid and regulate the temperature by adjusting the upper and lower vents.

MEAT

Barbecued Beef Ribs

Serves 4

Ingredients

1½ kg (approx. 3 lb) beef ribs

Marinade

45 ml (1½ fl oz) soy sauce
120 ml (4 fl oz) olive oil
45 ml (1½ fl oz) hot mustard
20 ml (⅔ fl oz) lemon juice
½ teaspoon chilli powder
1 clove garlic, crushed
black pepper, to serve
1 onion, thickly sliced

Method

Cut ribs into serving pieces. Place in deep bowl.

Combine soy sauce, oil, mustard, lemon juice, chilli powder, garlic and pepper.

Pour marinade over ribs, and wedge a few slices of thick onions between pieces of beef.

Marinate for 24 hours, turning from time to time.

Barbecue over hot coals for about 20 minutes or until done.

Serve with barbecue sauce.

Korean Barbecue Beef Ribs

Serves 4–6

Ingredients

12 beef ribs, 7 cm (just under 3 in) long

Marinade

360 ml (12 fl oz) soy sauce
45 g (1½ oz) sesame seeds, toasted
3 teaspoons sugar
1 teaspoon chilli
3 large cloves garlic, crushed

Method

Place the ribs in large plastic bag.

Combine the soy sauce, sesame seeds, sugar, chilli and garlic and pour over the ribs.

Press the air out of the bag and tie the top securely.

Refrigerate for 4 hours, turning the bag over occasionally.

Remove ribs and barbecue 10 cm (4 in) above the hot coals for about 15 minutes, or until the ribs are brown and crisp.

Turn the ribs over occasionally.

Jardi

Flanken Cut Short Barbecue Ribs

Serves 4–6

Ingredients

1.5 kg (3 lb) flanken cut short ribs
½ cup barbecue rub of your choice
1 tablespoon olive oil
½ cup barbecue sauce

Method

Rub the ribs, ensuring they are well coated with the dry mixture.

Place the ribs in a single layer on a tray.

Cover and refrigerate for at least 2 hours (overnight is better).

Place the ribs on a oiled hot to medium barbecue grill.

Cook for 6 minutes on each side, then reduce the heat to low.

Brush with the barbecue sauce on each side until sticky and well coated with the sauce.

Rest for a few minutes before serving.

Lamb Ribs

Serves 2–4

Ingredients

2 tablespoons olive oil
4 cloves of garlic, minced
2 sprigs fresh rosemary, finely chopped
2 teaspoons salt
2 teaspoons freshly cracked black pepper
1 kg (2 lb) lamb ribs, cut into 4 rib segments
2 cups woodchips, soaked in water (applewood is best for smoking lamb, or cherrywood if you can get it)

Method

Combine the oil, garlic, rosemary, salt and pepper in a bowl. Spread mixture evenly over lamb ribs so that the whole surface is coated.

Wrap lamb in cling film and let sit for an hour in the fridge.

Prepare your barbecue, light the coals and get the heat to 110°C (230°F).

Place a water filled drip tray next to the coals and place the cooking rack on top.

Place the lamb ribs on the cooking rack away from the direct heat of the coals.

Drop a handful of woodchips over the coals and place the lid on.

Cook the ribs for 4 hours, making sure the temperature stays at 110°C (230°F).

Remove lid and add a handful of woodchips to the hot coals every hour or so, replacing lid after each addition.

After 4 hours, move each rack of ribs over the coals and cook for 2 minutes a side, uncovered. This will burn most of the fat from the ribs.

Remove the ribs and wrap in foil, allow to sit for 15 minutes before eating the hell out of them!

Smokey Barbecue Spare Ribs

Serves 6–8

Ingredients

2 x 1 kg (2 lb) racks American-style ribs
¾ cup smokey barbecue relish
¼ cup olive oil

Method

Place the ribs in a large, non-metallic dish. Thoroughly combine the relish and the oil and liberally brush onto the ribs.

Cover and marinate in the refrigerator for several hours or overnight, turning occasionally.

Take 2 large sheets of heavy-duty foil and place on a work surface. Place a rack of ribs on each.

Generously cover both sides of ribs with extra marinade.

Wrap into a double-folded parcel, making sure all joins are well sealed to prevent leakage. Carefully place the parcel onto a tray, taking care not to tear the foil.

Refrigerate if not cooking immediately.

Prepare the barbecue for direct-heat cooking. Place a wire cake rack on the grill bars to stand 25 mm above the grill.

Place the foil parcels on the rack and cook for 10 minutes on each side, a total of 20 minutes.

Move the parcel to a plate. Open the foil and discard. Lift the ribs onto the rack.

Continue cooking and brush with extra relish, turning until ribs are well browned and crisp, this should take about 10 minutes.

Cut between the ribs to separate, pile onto a platter and serve immediately.

You must eat these as soon as they are cooked otherwise they will become dry and tough.

Barbecued Beef Ribs

Serves 2–4

Ingredients

1½ kg (3 lb) beef ribs

Marinade

2 tablespoons soy sauce
6 tablespoons olive oil
2 tablespoons hot mustard
1 tablespoon lemon juice
½ teaspoon chilli powder
1 clove garlic, crushed
black pepper
1 onion, thickly sliced

Method

Cut ribs into serving pieces. Place in deep bowl.

Combine soy sauce, oil, mustard, lemon juice, chilli powder, garlic and pepper.

Pour marinade over ribs, and wedge a few slices of thick onions between pieces of beef.

Marinate for 24 hours, turning from time to time.

Barbecue over hot coals for about 20 minutes or until done.

Serve with barbecue sauce.

Back ribs, short ribs, plate ribs, chuck ribs and, in my case broken ribs; there are many different cuts to choose from.

This recipe works best with back ribs.

Remember to let the meat reach room temperature before you throw it on the barbecue.

Honey-glazed Spare Ribs

Serves 4–6

Ingredients

2 kg (4 lb) pork spare ribs, trimmed of excess fat
2 onions, chopped
2 tablespoons fresh parsley, chopped
1 cup chicken stock
2 tablespoons lemon juice
125 g (4½ oz) butter, melted

Soy-Honey Marinade

4 small fresh red chillies, chopped
4 cloves garlic, chopped
2 spring onions, chopped
1 tablespoon fresh ginger, finely grated
1½ cup rice-wine vinegar
½ cup soy sauce
170 g (6 fl oz) honey

Method

To make the marinade, combine the chillies, garlic, spring onions, ginger, vinegar, soy sauce and honey in a non-metallic dish. Add ribs, toss to coat, cover and marinate in the refrigerator for at least 4 hours.

Drain the ribs and reserve the marinade.

Cook the ribs, basting occasionally with reserved marinade, on a hot barbecue grill for 8–10 minutes or until the ribs are tender and golden.

Place the remaining marinade in a saucepan, add the onions, parsley, stock and lemon juice and bring to the boil.

Reduce the heat and simmer for 15 minutes or until sauce reduces by half.

Pour the mixture into a food processor or blender and process to make a purée. With the motor running, pour in the hot melted butter and process to combine.

Serve the sauce with the spare ribs.

Smoked Pork Ribs

Serves 2–4

Ingredients

4 racks of pork ribs
2 cups cola
¼ cup cider vinegar
2 cups woodchips, soaked in water (applewood or hickory are best for smoking pork)
2 cups barbecue sauce

For the rub

½ cup brown sugar
2 tablespoons garlic powder
2 tablespoons salt
2 tablespoons cumin
2 tablespoons sweet paprika
2 teaspoons cayenne pepper

Method

Mix the rub ingredients together. Apply rub to the ribs so that they are completely coated in the mixture.

Wrap the ribs in cling film and refrigerate for 2–12 hours. The longer you leave them, the better they are.

Unwrap the ribs and place them in a plastic container. Pour the cola and vinegar over the top of the ribs and seal the container. Refrigerate for 12 hours.

Assemble some heat beads on only one side of your barbecue. Light the coals and get the heat to 110°C. Place a water filled drip tray next to the coals and set up the cooking rack. Place the ribs on the cooking rack away from the direct heat of the coals.

Drop a handful of woodchips over the coals and place the lid on the Weber.

Cook the ribs for 4 hours, maintaining a heat of 110°C.

Remove the lid and add a new handful of woodchips to the coals every hour or so.

After 4 hours, remove the lid from the barbecue and using a silicone basting brush or pastry brush, apply a thick coat of the Barbecue Sauce to the ribs.

Flip the ribs over and apply the barbecue sauce to the other side.

Repeat this flippin' and bastin' process every 15 minutes for the next hour.

Remove the ribs from the barbecue and wrap in foil.

Allow them to sit for 20 minutes before tucking in.

Satay Sauce

Serves 4–6

Ingredients

½ teaspoon ground ginger
½ teaspoon ground coriander
¼ teaspoon ground cumin
½ onion, grated
2 tablespoons peanut oil
1 teaspoon freshly crushed garlic
¾ cup roasted peanuts, puréed into a paste
2 teaspoons tomato paste
¾ cup creamed coconut
3 tablespoons honey
¼ teaspoon salt

Method

Tip all the spices into a dry skillet and fry gently, stiring constantly until they begin to smoke.

Remove from the heat and continue to stir for another minute.

Add the grated onion and quickly combine.

Return to the heat and add the peanut oil.

Gently fry the spices and onion for 3–4 minutes, then add the garlic.

Fry for 1 minute, then add all other ingredients.

Simmer for 10 minutes.

Allow to cool, then transfer to an airtight container.

Makes approximately 2 cups in finished volume.

Can be stored in the refrigerator for approximately 1 week.

Skirt Steak Satays

Serves 6–8

Ingredients

1 skirt steak, about 700 g (1½ lb)
2 tablespoons vegetable oil
1 tablespoon lime or lemon juice
salt and pepper to taste
½ cup of satay sauce
juice of ½ lemon
1 tablespoon peanut oil
20 long satay sticks, soaked for 30 minutes in cold water

Method

Place the skirt steak on a chopping board. Remove any membrane.

With a large knife lightly score the surface in a diagonal criss-cross pattern on both sides. This has a tenderising effect as it cuts through the meat fibres; it also speeds up absorption of the marinade.

Mix the oil, lime juice, salt and pepper together. Place the steak in a flat, non-metallic dish. Pour in the oil mixture, turn the meat to coat both sides.

Marinate for 2 hours, turning once.

Remove from the marinade, pat dry and place on a cutting board.

Slice the steak across the grain, with knife held at a 45-degree angle to the meat. Strips should be about 12 cm long, 2 cm wide and 3 mm thick.

Weave the strips onto the soaked satay sticks and gently spread them out flat, not bunched up. Arrange the skewers in a non-metallic flat dish, a lasagna dish for example. Combine the lemon juice, satay sauce and peanut oil to form a marinade. Pour over the skewers.

Marinate for 30 minutes.

Prepare the barbecue for direct-heat cooking, high heat. Oil the grill bars well. Slip a double foil band under the exposed part of the skewers to protect them from burning.

Arrange the satays and cook for 1–2 minutes per side.

Pork Skewers

Serves 4–6

Ingredients

1½ kg (3 lb) boneless shoulder of pork
1 cup Teriyaki sauce
1½ cups Greek-style yoghurt
8–10 bamboo skewers, soaked in water for 30 minutes
spring onions, sliced, to serve
½ cup chunky tomato relish

Method

Cut the pork into 25 mm cubes. Place the cubes in a bowl and pour over the sauce to coat well, but keep a little to brush with while cooking.

Cover and marinate in refrigerator for 1–2 hours or overnight to tenderise.

Prepare the barbecue for direct-heat cooking and heat to hot.

Turn a gas barbecue down to medium–hot when food is placed on.

Place the pork skewers on the grill.

Cook, turning and brushing with extra sauce for 12–15 minutes or until cooked to your liking.

Serve skewers with spring onions scattered on top with chunky tomato relish in a dipping bowl.

Lamb Kebabs

Serves 4–6

Ingredients

750 g (1½ lb) boneless lamb cut into 2 cm (1 in) cubes
½ cup lemon juice
2 teaspoons fresh oregano
1 tablespoon fresh parsley, finely chopped
2 bay leaves, torn
1 small onion, chopped
¼ cup olive oil
ground black pepper
8 bamboo skewers, soaked

For Serving

2 packets pocket pita breads
2 tubs tabouli
1 bottle chilli and garlic sauce

Method

Place the lamb cubes in a bowl with the remaining ingredients. Mix to coat the lamb well.

Cover and marinate in refrigerator for 2 hours or more.

Thread 5–6 pieces of lamb onto each skewer. Retain the marinade.

Place kebabs on a tray. Take to barbecue area with breads, tabouli and remaining marinade.

Prepare the barbecue grill or hotplate for direct-heat cooking. Heat to high and oil well. Place on the kebabs.

Cook and turn when needed. Baste frequently with the remaining marinade.

Cook for 4–6 minutes on each side. Do not overcook. Meat should feel springy when pressed. Place the pocket pita breads at the side of the barbecue plate to warm up.

Serve on a pita bread and spoon in a good serving of tabouli, add kebab skewer and a squeeze of the chilli and garlic.

Barbecue Meatball Skewer

Serves 2–4

Ingredients

oil, for cooking of your choice
1 onion, finely diced
500 g (18 oz) beef mince
1 egg
2 bacon rashers, finely diced
1 tablespoons barbecue sauce
1 tablespoons Worcestershire sauce
1 garlic clove, crushed
50 g (1¾ oz) panko breadcrumbs
salt and black pepper, to season

Method

If using bamboo skewers, soak in water for 20 minutes.

Heat some oil in a frying pan over medium heat.

Add the bacon and the onion then cook until the onion is soft and golden.

Combine the remaining ingredients, ensuring that it is well combined, then roll into golf size balls.

Place four balls on each skewer.

Place the skewers on a medium–high barbecue flatplate and cook for 8–12 minutes or until golden brown, turning every few minutes to brown all sides.

Serve with salad and coleslaw or place the meatballs on a long bread roll with dressing of your choice.

T-Bone and Herb Butter

Serves 4

Ingredients

4 large T-bone steaks
olive oil, for cooking
salt and pepper, to season
parmesan, garlic and parsley butter

Method

Remove the steaks from the fridge and leave for 20 minutes to come to room temperature.

Brush the steaks with olive oil and season with salt and pepper.

Cook on a medium–high barbecue for 3–4 minutes on each side for a rare to medium steak, or until cooked to your liking.

Serve the steaks with a slice of the parmesan, garlic and parsley butter.

Parmesan, Garlic and Parsley Butter

Serves 2–4

Ingredients

100 g (3½ oz) softened butter
3 tablespoons finely grated parmesan cheese
1 garlic clove, crushed
2 tablespoons chopped flat-leaf parsley
salt and pepper, to taste

Method

Mix the ingredients in a bowl until smooth.

Place the mixture onto a piece of plastic wrap and roll into a tube shape, twisting the ends and tie.

Place in the freezer until firm, then cut into slices just before use.

T-bone Steak

Serves 4

Ingredients

80 g (2¾ oz) butter, softened
3 cloves garlic, crushed
1 teaspoon Piri Piri seasoning
1 teaspoon parsley flakes
4 T-bone steaks, about 300 g (10 oz) each
olive oil
salt and freshly ground black pepper

Method

Combine the butter, garlic, Piri Piri seasoning and parsley in a bowl. Mix together until smooth.

Place the mixture onto cling wrap and roll into a tube shape.

Place in the refrigerator or freezer until firm.

Brush the steaks with olive oil and season with salt and pepper.

Cook the steaks on the barbecue grill for 3 minutes each side or until cooked to your liking.

Serve the steaks with crispy potatoes.

It is important to bring meat up to room temperature for 20–30 minutes.

Season well with salt and pepper on both sides.

Steak with Pepper Sauce

Serves 1 per rump steak

Ingredients

500 g (18 oz) rump steak, trimmed
freshly ground black pepper
salt, to taste
pepper sauce
1½ teaspoons drained green peppercorns
½ cup fresh parsley, chopped
½ cup fresh chives, chopped
knob of butter
¼ cup cream

Method

Prepare the barbecue and ensure it has a high heat.

Place the rump steak on the grill and lightly sprinkle with pepper.

Cook until lightly browned, then turn and lightly sprinkle the other side with pepper.

To make the sauce, fry the peppercorns, parsley and chives with a knob of butter in the pan over a medium heat.

Then add the cream. If you want a lot of sauce, add all the cream. If only a little sauce is required, add only half the quantity.

Serve the rump steak with sauce on the side, season with salt to taste.

Rib Eye with Chimichurri

Serves 1

Ingredients

rib eye fillets, on the bone – one for each person
salt and black pepper, to season
1 small red chilli, finely sliced, to garnish

Chimichurri Recipe

½ bunch coriander, leaves finely chopped
½ bunch flat-leaf parsley, finely chopped
2 garlic cloves, crushed
1 green chilli, finely diced
juice and zest of 1 lemon
3 tablespoons olive oil

Method

Preheat the barbecue grill plate to high heat.

Season the steaks with salt and pepper on both sides.

Place the steaks on the grill and cook to your liking.

To make the chimichurri, combine the coriander, parsley, garlic, green chilli, lemon juice and zest and oil in a bowl.

Serve the steaks with the chimichurri and a sprinkle of red chilli.

Drunken Sirloin Steaks

Serves 4

Ingredients

4 bone-in sirloin steaks

Marinade

180ml (6 fl oz) beer
2 cloves garlic, crushed
60ml (2 fl oz) Worcestershire sauce
60ml (2 fl oz) tomato sauce
oil for cooking

Method

Trim steaks of any visible fat. Place beer, garlic, Worcestershire sauce and tomato sauce in a large shallow ceramic or glass dish and mix to combine.

Add steaks to marinade, turn to coat, cover and set aside to marinate at room temperature for at least 3 hours, or in the refrigerator overnight. Turn occasionally during marinating.

Preheat the barbecue to hot.

Drain steaks and reserve marinade. Cook steaks on lightly oiled barbecue, brushing with reserved marinade, for 3–5 minutes each side or until cooked to your liking. Serve immediately

Marinated Barbecue Steak with Chimichurri

Serves 1

Ingredients

sirloin steaks – one per person
3 red onions, cut into wedges
3 tomatoes, cut into wedges
60ml (2 fl oz) olive oil
60ml (2 fl oz) red wine vinegar
1 teaspoon dried oregano
1 teaspoon sweet paprika
salt and freshly ground black pepper
chimichurri sauce, to serve

Chimichurri Recipe

½ bunch coriander, leaves finely chopped
½ bunch flat-leaf parsley, finely chopped
2 garlic cloves, crushed
1 green chilli, finely diced
juice and zest of 1 lemon
3 tablespoons olive oil

Method

Place steaks, onions and tomatoes in a large shallow ceramic dish.

Combine olive oil, red wine vinegar, dried oregano, sweet paprika, salt and pepper in a jug. Pour over steaks, onions and tomatoes cover with plastic wrap and place in the fridge to marinate for 30 minutes.

Remove steaks from marinade.

Cook steaks, onions and tomatoes on a barbecue plate or grill for 3 minutes each side or until cook to your liking.

Serve steaks with onion wedges, tomato wedges, chimichurri sauce and salad.

Pork Steaks with Mushroom Sauce

Serves 4

Ingredients

1 tablespoon vegetable oil
4 pork shoulder steaks, trimmed of excess fat
freshly ground black pepper

Mushroom sauce

350 g (10½ oz) closed cup mushrooms, sliced
1 clove garlic, crushed
1 teaspoon paprika
300 ml (10 fl oz) beef stock
1 tablespoon redcurrant jelly
1 tablespoon tomato purée
teaspoons cornflour
1 tablespoon water
2 tablespoons half-fat crème fraîche

Method

Heat the barbecue to a high heat and oil the grill. Season the pork steaks with pepper and sear for 1 minute on each side to brown, then cook for a further 5 minutes on each side or until tender and cooked through.

Remove and keep warm.

To make the sauce, place the mushrooms and garlic in a fry pan and fry for 2 minutes or until softened. Stir in the paprika, beef stock, red currant jelly and tomato purée.

Bring to the boil, then simmer for 5 minutes or until reduced slightly.

Mix the cornflour with the water to form a paste, stir into the sauce and simmer for a further 2 minutes or until the sauce has thickened.

Take of the heat and then stir in the crème fraîche.

Serve the pork steaks with the sauce on the side and with your favourite salads or vegetables.

Surf and Turf

Serves 4

Ingredients

4 lobster tails
90 g (3 oz) butter melted
4 teaspoons minced garlic
30 g (1 oz) plain flour
60 ml (2 fl oz) dry white wine
240 ml (8 fl oz) milk
60 ml (2 fl oz) cream
1 teaspoon fresh basil, chopped finely
¼ bunch fresh parsley, chopped finely
salt and pepper to taste
4 pieces thick steak, approx. 2½ cm (1 in) whichever cut you like best

Mashed Potatoes

500 g (18 oz) potatoes, peeled and chopped
1 good size sweet potato, peeled and chopped
1 tsp fresh chives
60 ml (2 fl oz) milk or cream
60 g (2 oz) butter, room temperature
salt and pepper, to taste

Asparagus

16 spears of fresh asparagus
olive oil
salt and pepper, to taste

To make the surf sauce; melt butter and stir in garlic – cook for 2 mins, don't allow garlic to brown. Then add flour, stirring all the time and cook for a minute or so then whisk in wine with a hand whisk.

Method

Heat slowly, whisking the whole time to keep sauce smooth, slowly adding milk until all used (use less or more according to thickness).

Heat and keep whisking, simmering, until it is to the thickness you require.

Then stir in the cream, herbs and seasonings. Bring back to simmer and bring to consistency you prefer.

With kitchen scissors, cut each side of the soft shell of the underside of the lobster tails and remove.

Run a metal skewer through the length of each tail to keep them flat while cooking.

Place the lobster tails cut side down and cook for minutes to sear the meat on the barbecue.

Turn over to shell side down and cook for 5–8 minutes until the shell turns red and the meat is white and firm, but not dry.

To make the mashed potato; boil the potato and sweet potato till tender, then mash together with the seasonings.

Stir in the milk and butter until smooth.

For the asparagus; and boil, steam or barbecue the asparagus until tender/crisp – about 5 minutes or so, depending on their size – then toss through seasonings & olive oil.

Keep the mashed potatoes and the asparagus warm. When you're ready to eat; cook the steaks to your taste (medium rare is best of course!)

To assemble; place a dollop of mash in the centre of each plate and lay 4 spears of asparagus to the side of each.

Place the steak on the mash and ladle over some sauce.

Place the lobster on top and serve immediately.

Barbecue Flattened Lamb Leg

Serves 2–4

Ingredients

1.5 kg (2 lb) lamb leg
2 garlic cloves, crushed
1 rosemary sprig, roughly chopped
2 tablespoons roughly chopped thyme leaves
3 tablespoons olive oil
½ tablespoon paprika
salt and black pepper, to season
3 lemons (1 to juice and 2 cut in half to garnish)

Method

Cut the lamb from the bone and cut to spread out flat (ask your butcher to do this to save time).

Combine the lamb and all of the ingredients except the lemon halves in a large ziplock bag. Leave to marinate for at least 4 hours (overnight is better).

Remove the lamb from the bag and using skewers, flatten out the lamb for cooking.

Place the lamb on a medium barbecue grill, turning every 5 minutes, and cook for approximately 25–30 minutes for medium– rare or until cooked to your liking.

Remove and cover with foil.

Allow to the lamb to rest for 10 minutes before slicing.

Slice the lamb and place on a serving dish and grilled lemon halves.

Squeeze the lemon onto the lamb at the table just before serving.

Roast Beef Special

Serves 4–6

Ingredients

1 boneless sirloin roast, about 1½ kg (3 lb)
ground black pepper

Horseradish Mustard Butter

250 g (9 oz) butter, softened
2 tablespoons horseradish cream
2 tablespoons Dijon mustard
1 tablespoon finely chopped fresh parsley
300 g (10 oz) medium–sized potatoes, scrubbed and wrapped in foil

Method

Trim off some of the fat from the roast, leaving a thin layer. Season with pepper, set aside.

Place the softened butter in a bowl and beat lightly with a wooden spoon.

Add the horseradish cream, mustard and parsley. Mix to combine.

Place into a butter crock or suitable dish. Cover and chill until required.

Prepare the barbecue for indirect cooking. Place a drip pan in the centre. For a charcoal kettle barbecue, heat to medium. For a gas kettle or covered gas barbecue heat to hot.

Place the roast beef on the grill directly over drip pan and cook for 1–1½ hours until the beef is cooked to your liking.

Add foiled wrapped potatoes to the barbecue after 1 hour. Place them on the direct heat each side of meat.

Turn every 10–15 minutes. Test with a skewer and remove when done.

When the roast is cooked transfer to a carving platter.

Cover loosely with foil and stand for 10 minutes to rest before carving.

Serve carved in thick slices, topped with the horseradish mustard butter with potatoes and a side salad.

Honey Pork Roast

Serves 4–6

Ingredients

2–2.5 kg (5 lb) boneless pork leg
¾ cup honey
1 tablespoon freshly chopped chilli (optional)
zest of 1 lemon
1 kg (2¼ lb) potatoes, peeled and cut into wedges
1½ teaspoons lemon pepper
1 teaspoon freshly crushed garlic
¼ cup oil
⅓ cup water
1 head radicchio lettuce

Method

To make the glaze, combine the honey, chilli and lemon zest. Brush the surface of the meat generously with the glaze. Refrigerate, covered, until ready to use. Stand at room temperature for 20 minutes before cooking.

Place the potato wedges in a foil tray. Mix the lemon pepper, garlic, oil and water together. Pour over the potatoes.

Cut the radicchio in half lengthwise. Cut each half into 3 wedges. Insert a small bamboo skewer from the centre of outside edge to the centre of the thin wedge edge to keep them from falling apart.

Prepare a covered barbecue for indirect-heat cooking, charcoal to medium high and gas to high, turned down to medium when the food is placed in.

Place the meat on the well-oiled bars over the drip tray. Place the potatoes next to the roast over indirect heat. Brush the roast with the glaze, close the cover and cook for 60 minutes.

Move the tray of potatoes over the direct heat and turn the potatoes. Brush the roast again with glaze, close hood and continue to cook for 1 hour, brushing the roast with glaze every 15 minutes.

When the potatoes are browned, remove and keep hot. The roast is cooked when the juices run clear when pricked with a skewer, or the internal temperature on a meat thermometer is about 68°C (155°F) for medium–well done. Remove roast onto a platter. Rest for 15 minutes.

Reheat the potatoes. Brush both sides of the radicchio wedges with the marinade and grill over direct heat for 3–5 minutes, brushing with the glaze.

Moroccan Lamb

Serves 4–6

Ingredients

12 lamb cutlets, Frenched
2 teaspoons olive oil
Moroccan spice mix seasoning

Couscous

1½ cups instant couscous
1½ cups boiling water
½ teaspoon salt
1 tablespoon butter
5 dried apricot halves
2 tablespoons slivered almonds, toasted

Method

Rub cutlets with a little oil on both sides and sprinkle on both sides with the Moroccan seasoning. Place on a platter, cover and refrigerate for 20 minutes. Stand at room temperature for 15 minutes before cooking.

While lamb is standing, place the couscous in a large bowl. Bring water and salt to the boil and pour immediately over the couscous. Stir, then stand covered for 5 minutes or until all water is absorbed.

Line the steamer with a circle of baking paper larger than the base.

With a skewer punch through the paper to make some holes to enable steam to enter.

Spoon the couscous into the steamer. Sprinkle on the apricots, set the steamer over a skillet of boiling water and steam uncovered for 20 minutes.

Add the butter and almonds and fork through.

Prepare the barbecue for direct-heat cooking. Place the steamer at the side of hot plate to keep hot.

Place the cutlets on hottest part of the grill.

Cook for 2 minutes. Move to second zone of grill and cook 2 minutes more. Turn cutlet with tongs, return to hotter grill and cook second side likewise.

Tip the steamer with the couscous on its side next to serving platter and pull out the paper, tipping the couscous onto the platter.

Mound it high, arrange the cutlets around the couscous and serve immediately.

Flank Steak Tacos

Serves 2–4

Ingredients

1 kg (2¼ lb) flank steak
3 tablespoons barbecue rub
2 tablespoons olive oil
1 tablespoon apple cider vinegar
6 x 15 cm (6 in) soft tacos
coriander, to garnish
1 lime, cut into wedges, to serve
1 jalapeño, finely sliced (optional)

Method

Rub the flank steaks with the barbecue rub and place in a bowl or plastic bag with the olive oil and vinegar allow to marinate for at least 30 minutes at room temperature (overnight in the fridge will give better (results).

Cook the steaks on a medium–high barbecue grill for 3–4 minutes on each side for medium rare–medium, or to your liking.

Rest for 4 minutes, then slice into strips against the grain.

While the steak is resting, warm the soft taco on the grill (on low or turned off, depending on the heat of your grill).

Serve the tacos with the flank steak and salsa and some lime wedges on the side.

Garnish with coriander. Add extra jalapeños if you are game.

Salsa

Serves 2–4

Ingredients

1 red onion or white onion, diced
2 tomatoes, diced
¼ bunch coriander, roughly chopped
juice of 1 lime salt, to season

Method

To make the salsa, combine the onion, tomatoes, coriander, lime juice and salt, to taste, in a bowl.

Refrigerate until needed.

Beer-marinated Lamb Rack

Serves 4–6

Ingredients

1–3 racks (allow 3 –4 chops per person)
200 ml (7 fl oz) pale ale, or your beer of choice
1 tablespoon brown sugar
1 rosemary sprig
salt, to season
1 tablespoon cracked black pepper

Method

Combine the ale, sugar, rosemary and salt and pepper and mix until the sugar is dissolved.

Place lamb in the marinade for at least 30 minutes at room temperature (1–2 hours would be better with the meat at room temperature for the last 30 minutes).

Remove the racks from the marinade and pat dry with paper towel.

Grill the lamb rack, fat side down, for approximately 5 minutes on a medium–high temperature with the lid open.

Turn the lamb rack over and cook for an additional 5 minutes for medium–rare with the lid down. Cook for longer if you like your lamb cooked more, or the racks you have are bigger.

Remove from the grill and rest for 5 minutes, then cut into individual chops.

Serve immediately.

Short Loin Lamb

Serves 4–6

Ingredients

12 thick lamb short loin chops
¾ cup honey
1 teaspoon garlic
2 tablespoons soy sauce

Salsa

5 limes
2 medium-sized red onions, finely diced
1 cup coarsely chopped rocket leaves
½ teaspoon sugar, or to taste
salt, to taste
1 teaspoon chopped fresh chilli

Method

Place the chops in a large, non-metallic dish on one layer.

Cover with the soy sauce, garlic and honey and marinate for 3–4 hours in refrigerator. Stand at room temperature 20 minutes before cooking.

While lamb is marinating prepare the salsa, peel the limes, removing all pith, cut in half lengthwise. Remove core and cut into 5 mm cubes.

Toss the cubed lime, onions, chopped rocket, chilli and sugar together.

Add salt to taste, place in a bowl and sprinkle with freshly ground black pepper.

Refrigerate until serving time.

Prepare the barbecue for two-zone direct-heat cooking. Oil the grill well.

Place the meat on the hottest part of the grill in rows and cook for 4 minutes, brushing with the extra marinade twice.

Turn the chops, brush with extra marinade, move to second zone to complete cooking until done to your liking.

Total cooking time is 6–8 minutes for medium.

If marinade is charring, place a sheet of baking paper over the grill and place the chops on the baking paper.

Serve with salsa and accompany with barbecued baby sweetcorn or other vegetables of your choice.

Honey-Glazed Pork Cutlets

Serves 2–4

Ingredients

4 pork loin cutlets
175 g (6 fl oz) store-bought honey, garlic and soy marinade
sprig of rosemary, to serve
3 Roma or plum tomatoes

Method

Place the pork cutlets on a flat platter.

Brush each side with the marinade.

Stand for 30 minutes before cooking.

Heat the barbecue grill to hot. Coat well with oil spray.

Place the chops on the grill and cook for 4 minutes each side or to your liking, brushing with the marinade as they cook.

Serve the chops with the sprig of rosemary and the fresh tomatoes.

Make sure your loin cutlets are nice and thick as thin cuts are usually very lean, easily overcooked and can dry out easily.

Marinated Barbecue Pork Chops

Serves 2–4

Ingredients

4 pork chops

Marinade

3 tablespoons soy sauce
3 tablespoons Worcestershire sauce
3 tablespoons hoisin barbecue sauce
1 tablespoon balsamic vinegar
1 teaspoon garlic powder
1 teaspoon onion powder
salt and pepper, to taste

Method

Trim the pork chops of rind and excess fat.

Place all the marinade ingredients into a large zip-lock bag. Add the pork chops and marinade for 1–2 hours or longer if possible.

Heat the barbecue grill, then cook the chops for 5–6 minutes on each side. For crosshatch grill marks, turn 45 degrees after 3 minutes.

Turn down the grill and baste with the leftover marinade until the chops are cooked through.

When done, cover with foil and rest for 5 minutes before serving.

Pulled Pork Sandwich

Serves 6–10

Ingredients

2 onions, sliced
3 bay leaves
4 teaspoons mustard powder
4 teaspoons smoked paprika
1½–2 kg (3–4 lb) pork shoulder, boned with rind attached and tied (ask your butcher to do this)
150 g (5 oz) tomato sauce
90 ml (3 fl oz) red wine vinegar
20 ml (⅔ fl oz) Worcestershire sauce
12 teaspoons soft dark brown sugar
2 french sticks, sliced into rolls, and coleslaw to serve

Method

Heat oven to 160°C (320°F). Add onions and bay leaves to a large roasting tin. Mix mustard powder, paprika and 1 teaspoon of ground black pepper with a good pinch of salt. Thoroughly rub this all over the pork.

Place the pork, rind side up, on top of onions.

Pour 210 ml (7 fl oz) water in to the bottom of the tin, wrap well with foil and bake for 4 hours.

Light the barbecue. Mix tomato sauce, vinegar, Worcestershire sauce and brown sugar. Remove pork from tin and pat dry.

Place the roasting tin on the hob, add tomato sauce mixture and bubble for 10–15 minutes until thick and glossy.

Remove bay leaves and pour into a food processor; blitz until smooth. Smear half the sauce mixture onto the meat.

Once the barbecue flames have died down, cook the pork, skin side down, for 15 minutes until nicely charred, then flip and cook for another 10 minutes.

The meat will be very tender, so be careful not to lose any between the bars.

Lift the pork onto a large plate or tray. Remove string and skin. Using 2 forks, shred the meat into chunky pieces.

Add 60–90 ml (2–3 fl oz) of barbecue sauce and toss everything well to coat.

Pile into rolls and serve with extra sauce and a little coleslaw.

Nut-Crusted Lamb Racks

Serves 4

Ingredients

lamb racks (3–4 cutlets each)
2 cups soft white breadcrumbs
2 tablespoons melted butter
½ cup macadamia or brazil nuts, chopped
1 teaspoon fresh oregano
1 tablespoon fresh basil, finely chopped
1 tablespoon fresh parsley, finely chopped
½ teaspoon lemon pepper
1 egg, beaten
slender sweet potatoes
small onions, peeled and quartered with root end attached
1 tablespoon olive oil

Method

Trim some of the fat from the racks, leaving only a thin layer.

Place the breadcrumbs into a bowl. Add the butter, nuts, oregano, basil, parsley and lemon pepper. Mix to distribute ingredients evenly, then add enough egg to just bind the mixture (not too moist). Press firmly onto each rack.

Place in a tray, cover carefully with cling wrap, refrigerate.

Peel the sweet potato and cut diagonally into 2 cm slices. Place the sweet potato and onions in a foil roasting pan and drizzle with a little oil.

Prepare a covered barbecue for indirect cooking. Heat coals to medium high, gas barbecue to high.

Reduce heat to medium when food is placed. Place the foil tray with the sweet potato and onions on indirect heat, cover with lid or hood and cook for 15 minutes.

Open lid, move the potato tray to direct heat and turn the vegetables.

Place the lamb racks in the foil tray over indirect heat or place directly onto the grill bars over a drip tray.

Cover with hood and cook for 35 minutes.

Remove the lamb when done and rest 10 minutes before serving. Remove vegetables.

Serve the lamb racks on heated plates with a serving of vegetables.

Leg of Lamb

Serves 4–6

Ingredients

1½ kg (approx. 3 lb) boneless leg of lamb, butterflied
45 g (1½ oz) fresh rosemary leaves, roughly chopped
4 teaspoons celery salt
½ teaspoon black pepper, freshly ground
½ teaspoon coriander (cilantro) powder
½ teaspoon mild Indian curry powder
olive oil

Method

Lay the leg of lamb out as flat as possible and ensure that the meat has an even thickness. This can be difficult as the muscle structure varies and so you may have to slice the meat to flatten it. Skewer into place to maintain a flat appearance.

Mix the rosemary, salt, pepper, coriander (cilantro) and curry powder together. With your fingers, sprinkle/spread half the rub ingredients over the cut side of the lamb and then massage it in.

Put the leg of lamb onto a medium–hot barbecue grill cut-side down.

Cook for five minutes.

Lightly brush the skin side of the lamb with oil and turn the leg over to cook for 10–15 minutes with the hood down.

Brush the partially cooked cut side with a little oil and sprinkle over the remaining rub.

Turn the meat over again, drop the hood, and leave to cook on the skin side for 10 minutes.

Turn the leg one more time to the open flesh side and cook for a further 10–15 minutes with the hood down.

Remove from the barbecue and let rest for five minutes.

Slice the meat and serve with salads or vegetables of your choice.

Barbecued Port-glazed Lamb

Serves 6–8

Ingredients

2½ kg (5 lb 8 oz) leg of lamb
250 ml (9 fl oz) port
375 ml (13 fl oz) water

Port Glaze

4 tablespoons Dijon mustard
2 teaspoons finely grated orange rind
½ teaspoon grated nutmeg
375 ml (13 fl oz) port wine
125ml (4 fl oz) honey
2 tablespoons balsamic vinegar

Method

Preheat covered barbecue to a medium heat.

Place lamb on a wire rack set in a roasting tin and brush with glaze. Pour port wine and water into roasting tin, cover barbecue with lid and cook for 2 hours, brushing with glaze at 15 minute intervals, or until cooked to your liking.

To make the port glaze, place mustard, orange rind, nutmeg, port wine, honey and vinegar in a saucepan, bring to simmering over a low heat and simmer until mixture thickens and reduces slightly.

Veal Cutlet Parmigiana

Serves 4

Ingredients

4 veal cutlets, 1–1½ cm (⅓–½ in) thick
2 teaspoons olive oil
1 clove garlic, crushed
salt and pepper
2 Roma tomatoes, diced
½ teaspoon sugar
3 scallions (spring onions), finely sliced
1 tablespoon parsley, finely chopped
6 tablespoons mozzarella cheese, grated

Method

Bring the cutlets to room temperature (about 15 minutes).

Mix the oil, garlic and seasonings together and rub into the cutlets on both sides.

Mix the diced tomato, sugar, green onion and parsley together, add salt and pepper to taste and set aside.

Preheat the grill for 5 minutes then cover the bottom plate with a sheet of baking paper. Place the cutlets on top, close the grill and cook for 5 minutes.

Open the grill and spoon a pile of tomato mixture on top of each cutlet.

Cover with a sheet of baking paper, close and cook until heated through (about 30 seconds).

Open the grill and lift the baking paper.

Top each cutlet with 1 tablespoon of grated mozzarella, replace the baking paper and cook for 10–15 seconds to melt the cheese.

Remove the paper, then close the lid for 3 seconds to sear the cheese.

Serve immediately

Teriyaki Pork Steaks

Serves 4

Ingredients

4 pork loin steaks
1 cup teriyaki marinade
100 g (3½ oz) snow peas
1 red bell pepper (capsicum), cut into 2 cm (¾ in) pieces
1 yellow bell pepper (capsicum), cut into 2 cm (¾ in) pieces
1 small bunch scallions (spring onions), sliced into 3 cm (1¼ in) lengths
watercress to garnish

Teriyaki Marinade

½ cup soy sauce
½ cup orange juice
½ cup brown sugar
2 teaspoons ground ginger
3 cloves garlic, crushed

Method

Place the steaks into a shallow dish and pour over ½ cup of the marinade to cover the steaks well. Cover and place into refrigerator for a few hours or over night.

Prepare the barbecue for direct heat cooking. Oil the grill well. Heat until hot. Place the pork steaks on the grill. Cook for 5–7 minutes on each side, brushing with extra marinade while they are cooking.

Brush all the vegetables with some of the marinade and cook on the grill until they are coloured and tender. Place each steak onto a dinner plate and top with the cooked vegetables. Garnish with the watercress.

To make the teriyaki marinade, combine all ingredients in a glass bowl and stir well. Soak meat for at least 2 hours, covered in the refrigerator. Marinade can be used for brushing over meat while cooking.

Lamb Rissoles

Serves 2–4

Ingredients

500 g (18 oz) lamb mince
1 small onion finely diced
45 g (1½ fl oz) breadcrumbs
30 g (1 oz) diced sweet chargrilled capsicum
1 egg
1 clove garlic finely chopped
1 teaspoon ground cumin
¼ bunch fresh mint, finely chopped (keep some for garnish)
spray oil for cooking

Method

Place the mince, onion, breadcrumbs, mint, garlic and cumin in the bowl and combine.

Season with salt and pepper.

Divide mince mixture into 6 portions the shape each portion into a patty.

Heat barbecue plate or chargrill over medium–low heat.

Spray both sides of rissoles with oil.

Cook, turning occasionally, for 12 to 15 minutes or until cooked through.

Serve on platter with a salad or make a burger.

BURGERS & ROLLS

Blue Cheese Stuffed Hamburger

Serves 3–5

Ingredients

1 tablespoon butter
1 brown onion, finely diced
1 garlic clove, crushed
1 kg (2¼ lb) beef mince
½ teaspoon salt
½ teaspoon cracked pepper
1 teaspoon Worcestershire sauce
1 tablespoon barbecue sauce
30 g (1 oz) panko breadcrumbs
1 egg
250 g (9 oz) blue cheese (cut into five 20 g slices)
5 soft burger bun of your choice, halved
1 baby cos lettuce
2–3 tomatoes, sliced
aïoli or caramelised onions, to serve

Method

Melt the butter in a frying pan over medium heat. Add the onion and garlic and sweatuntil golden. Allow to cool.

Combined the mince, onion and garlic, salt, pepper, Worcestershire sauce, barbecue sauce, panko breadcrumbs and egg in a bowl. Mix by hand until well mixed.

Separate the mix into five equal balls.

Separate each ball again into two equal balls and place a piece of blue cheese into the centre and mould into a patty. Flatten and ensure each patty is well sealed around the edges.

Place the patties on a medium–high barbecue flatplate and cook the patties for 3–4 minutes on each side or done to your liking.

Spread the top half of the burger bun with aïoli or caramelised onion. Add the patty, then the lettuce leaves and tomato.

Deluxe Hamburgers

Serves 7–14

Ingredients

Burger Patties

1 kg (2¼ lb) ground beef
1 large onion, grated or processed
½ cup dried breadcrumbs
½ teaspoon salt
¼ teaspoon pepper
3 tablespoons tomato sauce
2 tablespoons water

Buns and Suggested Fillings

14 hamburger buns
softened butter for spreading
1 lettuce, separated into leaves, washed and drained
1 bunch rocket, washed and drained
2 large onions, thinly sliced and cooked on the hotplate
sandwich cheese slices
1 cup tomato sauce

Method

Combine all the ingredients for the burger patties. Knead by hand to distribute evenly and make the texture finer. Rest for 20 minutes in the refrigerator. With wet hands, shape into 14 flat patties about 8 cm (3 in) in diameter. Prepare barbecue for direct-heat cooking.

Heat until hot. Oil the grill bars, place on the patties and cook for 5–6 minutes on each side. Brush with a little oil as they cook. Split the buns and lightly spread with softened butter. Place buttered side down on hotplate and toast to golden colour.

To assemble, place a lettuce leaf on bottom half of bun, top with cooked patty, tomato sauce, onions, cheese slice, rocket leaf and your choice of pickle or relish. Top with remaining bun.

Bacon-wrapped Scallop Slider

Serves 6–12

Ingredients

6 slices streaky bacon, cut in half lengthwise
12 large scallops, roe off (U15 size)
spray oil
1 lemon
12 small brioche buns

Method

In a barbecue prepared for indirect cooking at 200°C (390°F). Line a baking tray with baking paper and lay out the bacon in a single layer.

Bake until the bacon is just golden but still soft and pliable, about 10 minutes.

Remove and cool on some paper towel to remove excess oil.

Wrap a slice of bacon around each scallop and secure it with a toothpick.

Season with salt and pepper and squeeze lemon juice all over.

Return the tray to the barbecue and cook for 12–15 minutes or until the bacon is sizzling and crispy.

Slice the brioche buns in half.

To assemble your sliders, remove the toothpicks from the scallop, place on a bun, add some sauce and add the top bun and serve.

Chicken Schnitzel Burger

Serves 6–12

Ingredients

1 cup panko breadcrumbs
salt and pepper, to taste
2 eggs
500 g (18 oz) chicken breast fillets, cut into pieces to fit buns
1 tablespoon olive oil
whole egg mayonnaise
2 tomatoes, sliced
1 cup baby spinach
12 slider buns of your choice

Method

In a shallow bowl, combine the breadcrumbs, salt and pepper.

In another bowl, beat the two eggs.

Dip the chicken pieces in the beaten egg, shake off excess then dip into the breadcrumbs.

Prepare barbecue for direct-heat cooking. Heat until hot.

Oil the grill bars, cook the schnitzels until golden brown for 5–6 minutes on each side.

Slice your buns in half lengthwise and toast.

To assemble your sliders, spread on the mayonnaise on the bottom half of the buns, add a piece of schnitzel, a slice of tomato and the top of the bun. Hold together with cocktail stick.

Add a slice of crispy bacon if you want.

Greek Lamb Burger

Serves 6

Ingredients

500 g (18 oz) ground/minced lamb
1 small onion, finely diced
1 clove garlic, minced
1 teaspoon ground cumin
1 teaspoon ground coriander
1 egg
1 teaspoon chilli flakes (optional)
salt and pepper, to taste
1 tablespoon olive oil
1 Lebanese cucumber, finely sliced with vegetable peeler
garlic mayonnaise
2 Turkish pide loaves, cut into 12 rings

Method

Using a cookie cutter, cut out rounds from the bread to create your slider buns.

Place mince in a large bowl and mix together with the onion, garlic, cumin, coriander, egg, chilli flakes, if using, and season with salt and pepper.

Roll into small balls and flatten the patties to fit your buns.

Prepare barbecue for direct-heat cooking. Heat until hot.

Oil the grill bars, cook the lamb for 3–4 minutes each side or to your liking.

To assemble your sliders, add some lettuce to the bun, a cooked patty then a slice or two of tomato and cucumber.

Finally, add a dollop of garlic mayonnaise.

Place the bun on top and hold everything together with a cocktail stick.

Serve them while hot.

Cajun Chicken Roll with Avocado and Bacon

Serves 6–12

Ingredients

500 g (18 oz) skinless chicken thighs
1 tablespoon cumin
1 tablespoon ground coriander
1 tablespoon hot or mild paprika
salt and pepper, to taste
2 tablespoons olive oil
6 bacon rashes
mayonnaise, to serve
2 avocadoes, sliced
1 cup arugula/rocket
12 ciabatta slider buns

Method

Cut the chicken thighs into pieces to fit the slider bun.

In a bowl, combine the cumin, ground coriander, paprika, salt and pepper.

In a shallow dish, layer out the chicken and drizzle with oil then sprinkle the spices over the chicken and rub in well.

Prepare barbecue for direct-heat cooking. When hot oil the grill bars and cook the chicken for 4–5 minutes each side until firm.

While the chicken is cooking, fry the bacon on the plate of the barbecue until crispy.

Slice the buns in half lengthwise and toast them.

To assemble the sliders, dollop the bottom buns with mayonnaise, spread on some baby spinach leaves, a piece of chicken, sliced avocado and top with bacon and the bun. Hold them together with a cocktail stick.

Meatloaf Burger

Serves 6–12

Ingredients

250 g (½ lb) ground/minced beef
250 g (½ lb) ground/minced pork
250 g (½ lb) ground/minced lamb
¾ cup breadcrumbs
1 large white onion, diced
1 large egg
¼ cup tomato paste
1 teaspoon Worcestershire sauce
2 cloves garlic, minced
1 teaspoon chilli powder
1 teaspoon ground cumin
salt and pepper to taste
½ cup barbecue sauce
200 g (7 oz) (Swiss or Chedder) cheese, grated
12 slider buns of your choice

Method

In a large bowl, combine the meat, breadcrumbs, onion, egg, tomato paste, Worcestershire sauce, garlic and spices.

Shape into a loaf to fit the size of the buns on a baking tray covered with baking parchment/paper. You may need to make more than one loaf.

Place the meat loaf into a barbecue prepared for indirect cooking at 180°C for 35 minutes, brushing with the barbecue sauce at 25 minutes. Remove and rest for 10 minutes before slicing.

Slice meatloaf thickly and serve hot or cold. Slice the buns in half lengthways.

To assemble your sliders, add a slice of meatloaf, drizzle over some barbecue sauce and sprinkle with some grated cheese. Place on the top of the bun. Hold together with a cocktail stick.

You can serve with a sweet coleslaw if you like but I prefer to eat them on their own!

Barbecued Fish Burger

Serves 2–4

Ingredients

4 of firm white fish – approximately 125 g (4½ oz) each
4 tablespoons Thai-style seafood seasoning
4 round Turkish pide
90 g (3 oz) butter, softened
200 g (7 oz) green salad mix or shredded lettuce
4 tablespoons sweet chilli sauce
2 large tomatoes, sliced
225 g (8 fl oz) traditional tartare sauce
2 tablespoons finely chopped spring onions
dill sprigs, to garnish

Method

Place the fish fillets on a plate. Sprinkle both sides with seasoning.

Cut the pide bread in half. Spread lightly with the butter.

Prepare the filling ingredients. Take all to the barbecue area.

Prepare the barbecue for direct-heat cooking. Heat to medium–high heat. Grease the grill bars well.

Brush the fish with oil, place on the grill bars and cook for 3 minutes each side or until cooked through.

Place the pide on the barbecue, crust side down, to heat a little, turn butter side down to lightly toast.

To assemble, place the lettuce on the base of each portion of pide bread, drizzle very lightly with the chilli sauce if desired.

Top with 3 tomato slices.

Place on the grilled fish, top with tartare sauce and sprinkle with chopped spring onion and a sprig of dill.

Place on the top piece of pide.

Tuna Sliders

Serves 6–12

Ingredients

1 x 425 g (15 oz) tinned tuna in brine, drained
½ cup dried breadcrumbs
½ white onion, diced
2 tablespoons fresh parsley, finely chopped
2 teaspoons Dijon mustard
¼ cup mayonnaise
juice of half a lemon
1 teaspoon hot sauce (Tabasco or sriracha)
1 egg
1 tablespoon olive oil
salt and pepper, to taste
1 cup mixed salad leaves, torn
3–4 tomatoes, sliced
tartare sauce to serve
12 slider buns of your choice allowing 1–2 per person

Method

Combine the tuna, breadcrumbs, onion, parsley, mustard, mayonnaise, lemon juice, hot sauce and egg in a large bowl and mix until well combined.

Roll into small balls and flatten the patties to fit your buns. Spray oil on your flat plate or grill and turn grill up to medium heat. Cook the patties until brown, about 3–4 minutes each side and set aside on some kitchen towel to drain.

To assemble your sliders, slice your buns in half. Add some mixed salad leaves, a slice or two of tomato and the tuna patty. Dollop with some tartare sauce and add the top of the bun. Use a cocktail stick to hold the burger together.

Serve them hot.

You could also serve this with sweet chilli sauce instead of tartare, if you want some extra heat.

Chicken Breast Burger with Haloumi Cheese

Serves 3–6

Ingredients

3 skinless chicken breast fillets
2 eggplants (aubergines), cut into 1 cm round slices
½ teaspoon salt
½ teaspoon cracked pepper
2 tablespoons barbecue rub
2 tablespoons olive oil
6 haloumi slices
sweet chilli sauce, to taste
6 burger rolls of your choice
2 baby cos lettuce
3 tomatoes
1 large cucumber

Method

Using a sharp knife, slice the chicken breast horizontally into two even pieces.

Salt each eggplant slice. Once water beads of liquid form on the surface, rinse the eggplant pieces thoroughly to remove the salt.

Pat dry and spread out on a cutting board.

Combine the salt, pepper and barbecue rub. Rub each chicken fillet with the mix and olive oil, then place on a medium–high grill.

Cook for 3–5 minutes on each side, or until cooked through.

Meanwhile, place the slices of eggplant and haloumi on a medium–high oiled barbecue flatplate, turning when golden brown.

Cut the burger rolls in half, spread the base of the rolls with sweet chill sauce.

Add the chicken, eggplant and haloumi, then top with lettuce, tomato and cucumber to your liking.

Chilli Cheeseburger

Serves 6–12

Ingredients

1tablespoon butter
1 small brown onion, finely diced
1 clove garlic, minced
500 g (18 oz) best-quality ground/minced beef you can afford
1 egg
1 teaspoon Worcestershire sauce
salt and pepper
1 tablespoon olive oil
3–4 slices cheese (Swiss or Tasty), cut into 4 pieces
12 slider buns of your choice allowing 1–2 for each person
bottled chillies, such as pickled jalapenos or chipotle in adobo sauce, diced hot sauce, such as Tabasco or sriracha sauce (a Thai-style hot sauce)

Method

Melt the butter in a non-stick frying pan until bubbling. Sweat the onions and garlic in the fryingpan until golden.

Allow to cool.

Place mince in a large bowl and combine with the cooked onion, garlic, egg and Worcestershire sauce, and season to taste.

Roll into small balls and flatten the patties to fit your buns.

Heat the oil on the grill from low to medium and cook the patties for 2–3 minutes each side, or to your liking.

Set patties aside on a plate and cover each one with a slice of cheese.

Slice the buns in half lengthways and toast them if you like.

To assemble the sliders, add a cooked patty to the bottom half of the buns, add a teaspoon of diced chilli (or more if you like it hot) then add some hot sauce if you want an even hotter kick. Hold them together with a cocktail stick and serve them while hot.

Chicken, Bacon and Cheese Burger

Serves 6–12

Ingredients

3 skinless chicken breasts
salt and pepper to taste
1 teaspoon olive oil
12 slices streaky bacon, cut in half
12 slider buns of your choice
ranch dressing or mayonnaise, to serve
6 slices Swiss cheese, cut in half

Method

Season the chicken with salt and pepper and on a pre-heat grill or hotplate add 1 teaspoon of oil and cook the chicken for 7–8 minutes each side or until cooked.

Also on the grill or hotplate cook the bacon until crispy. Remove from the grill and allow to drain on some paper towel. Dice the chicken and bacon, mix together in a bowl and set aside.

Slice the buns in half. Spread the bottom of the buns with ranch dressing or mayonnaise. Add the chicken and bacon mixture and top each roll with a slice of cheese. Place the buns on the grill and add the cheese until it melts. Add the top bun and serve hot.

Beef Sliders with Cheese

Serves 6–12

Ingredients

1 tablespoon butter
1 small onion, finely diced
1 clove garlic, minced
500 g (18 oz) best-quality ground/minced beef you can afford
1 egg
1 teaspoon Dijon mustard
1 teaspoon Worcestershire sauce
salt and pepper
1 tablespoon olive oil
iceberg lettuce, sliced
3–4 slices cheese (Swiss or Tasty)
2 tomatoes, sliced
pickles
whole egg mayonnaise
12 slider buns of your choice allowing 1–2 for each person

Method

Prepare barbecue for direct-heat cooking.

Heat until hot. Melt the butter on the barbecue plate, cook the onion and garlic until golden then allow to cool.

Place meat in a large bowl and mix in the cooked onion, garlic, egg, Worcestershire sauce and season with salt and pepper.

Roll into small balls and flatten the patties to fit your buns.

Slice the buns in half lengthways.

Spread the bottom halves of the buns with mayonnaise, add some lettuce, a cooked patty, a slice of cheese, tomato and cucumber and the top of the bun. Hold the buns together with cocktail sticks and serve while hot.

Turkey Burgers

Serves 6–12

Ingredients

2 tablespoons olive oil
1 small onion, finely diced
1 clove garlic, minced
500 g (18 oz) turkey
1 teaspoon Worcestershire sauce
salt and pepper, to taste
4–6 cheese slices (Swiss or Tasty), cut in half
12 strips streaky bacon
12 slider buns of your choice
mayonnaise
seeded or Dijon mustard

Method

Heat a tablespoon of oil in a frying pan on a medium heat.

Cook the onion and garlic in the pan until golden and allow to cool.

Place the turkey in a large bowl and add the cooked onion and garlic, Worcestershire sauce and season with salt and pepper.

Mix together until well-combined.

Roll into small balls and flatten the patties to fit your buns.

In a non-stick frying pan heat the rest of the oil and cook the patties for 3–4 minutes each side until brown.

Place a slice of cheese on top of each patty for the last minute of cooking.

While the patties are cooking, cook the bacon in another pan until crispy.

Slice the buns in half lengthwise.

Spread the bottom half of the buns with mayonnaise, add a cooked turkey patty with the melted cheese, a slice of bacon and a dollop of mustard on top.

Add the top of the bun and hold it together with a cocktail stick.

Serve while hot.

Steak Sandwich

Serves 4

Ingredients

Steak

500 g (18 oz) rump or sirloin steak (whichever you prefer)
pepper, freshly ground, to taste
salt, to taste

Sandwich

loaf of sliced sourdough
cup of rocket (arugula)
2 tomatoes, sliced
caramelised onion, to serve
mayonnaise, to serve

Method

Prepare barbecue for direct heat cooking on a high.

Season the steak with salt and pepper on both sides place the steak on the grill and cook to your liking.

Rest the steak while you toast sourdough on the grill.

Slice the steak then butter one side of the toasted sourdough.

Add the mayonnaise, rocket and tomato the season with salt and pepper to taste and top with the sliced steak and caramelised onion.

Place the other slice of sourdough on top and enjoy.

Prosciutto-wrapped Chipolata Roll

Serves 3–6

Ingredients

12 chipolata or cocktail sausages
12 thin slices prosciutto
1 teaspoon olive oil
1 tablespoon butter
tomato and chilli jam, to serve
6 dinner rolls

Method

Wrap the sausages in a single slice of prosciutto each.

Cook on the flat plate of your barbecue over a medium heat for 4–5minutes.

Turn down your barbecue to low and continue to cook ensuring that you don't burn the prosciutto for another 5minutes or until sausages are cooked.

Slice the rolls in half lengthways.

Add a sausage to each roll bun and top with some tomato and chilli jam.

Beef Sausage Hot Dog

Serves 8–16

Ingredients

8 beef sausages, linked
1 tablespoon butter
1 large onion, halved then sliced
salt and pepper, to taste
1 teaspoon olive oil
Dijon or yellow mustard, to serve
chives, for garnish (optional)
8–16 buns or dinner rolls

Method

Keeping the sausages linked, twist them in half to make two smaller sausages (16 in total) and then cut the links.

Prepare barbecue for direct-heat cooking. Melt the butter on the barbecue plate.

Add oil and the onion, and cook until golden.

Season to taste and set aside to use later.

On the barbecue heat the oil and cook the sausages to your liking.

When sausages are cooked split the roller bun lengthwise.

Add the sausage to the bun and top with the onion and mustard.

Sprinkle with chives just before serving.

Lamb Fillet Roll

Serves 6–12

Ingredients

1 teaspoon ground cumin
1 teaspoon sweet paprika
½ teaspoon cayenne pepper
salt, to taste
1–2 lamb fillets
1 tablespoon olive oil
12 buns of your choice
3 small tomatoes, thinly sliced
1 cup baby spinach leaves
½ cup feta, crumbed

Method

In a shallow dish combine cumin, paprika, cayenne pepper and salt to taste.

Coat the lamb fillet with the mixed spices.

Prepare barbecue for direct-heat cooking. Heat until hot. Oil the grill bars, cook the lamb for 3–4 minutes each side for medium or to your liking.

Remove from the heat and let the meat rest for 4 minutes before slicing the lamb diagonally into 1 cm slices.

Slice the buns in half lengthways.

Add the tomato, spinach, lamb and some feta before serving.

Steak and Blue Cheese on Turkish Bread

Serves 4

Ingredients

500 g (18 oz) flank steak
salt and freshly ground pepper, to taste
4 Turkish buns
200 g (3½ oz) blue cheese, crumbed
4 tablespoons mayonnaise
2 cups coleslaw

Method

Preheat the barbecue grill plate to high heat.

Season the steak with salt and pepper on both sides.

Place the steak on the grill and cook to your liking.

Remove the steak from the grill and rest it while toasting the ciabatta on the grill.

Slice the steak across the grain.

Butter one side of the toasted ciabatta with mayonnaise.

Top with coleslaw, then the sliced steak and some crumbed blue cheese.

Top with the other slice of ciabatta.

Serve immediately.

Kranksy Hotdog

Serves 4–6

Ingredients

6 Kranksy sausages
6 hot dogs rolls of your choice
cheddar, Swiss or provolone cheese, grated
caramelised onion relish
6 dinner rolls or hotdog rolls

Method

Slice the Kranksy sausages in half lengthways but not all the way through.

Place on the barbecue grill for 3–4 minutes on each side until heated through.

Place the Kranksy on the bread roll and top with the cheese and onion relish.

Lamb Cutlets wrapped in Prosciutto

Serves 4

Ingredients

12 frenched lamb cutlets
12 slices prosciutto
12 sage leaves
12 slices of shaved parmesan cheese

Method

Place a slice of Parmesan and a sage leave on each cutlet and then wrap in a slice of prosciutto.

Refrigerate until serving time.

Prepare the barbecue for two-zone direct-heat cooking. Oil the grill well.

Place the cutlets on the hottest part of the grill in rows and cook for 3–4 minutes, move to second zone to complete cooking until done to your liking.

Total cooking time is 8–10 minutes for medium.

Serve with salads or vegetables of your choice.

CHICKEN

Butterflied Lemon Chicken

Serves 6–8

Ingredients

1.2–1.5 kg (2½–3 lb) whole chicken, cut through the backbone
2 tablespoons Worcestershire sauce
salt
½ teaspoon cracked black pepper
1 garlic clove, crushed
juice and zest of 1 lemon
olive oil, for cooking

Method

Put the chicken on a chopping board, breast side down, and using a pair of kitchen scissors, cut closely through each side of the backbone.

Turn the chicken breast side up and open the chicken. Place your hand on top and flatten.

Rub the chicken with the Worcestershire sauce, salt, pepper, garlic, lemon and olive oil.

Place the chicken on the barbecue grill, breast side down, and cook over a medium–high heat for 15–20 minutes, depending on size.

Turn and cook for a further 15– 20 minutes.

Barbecue Chicken Drumsticks

Serves 4–6

Ingredients

12 chicken drumsticks

Marinade

60 ml (2 fl oz) tomato sauce
2–3 tablespoons lemon juice
2 tablespoons soy sauce
60 ml (2 fl oz) olive oil
½ teaspoon salt

Method

Grill chicken drumsticks over medium coals, turning frequently and basting with the marinade while cooking.

Cook until drumsticks are tender.

To make the marinade, combine marinade ingredients in a large bowl and mix together well.

Put chicken drumsticks into the bowl, cover and let stand for at least 20 minutes in the refrigerator.

Lollypop Chicken Sticks

Serves 4–6

Ingredients

500 g (18 oz) ground chicken meat
½ cup breadcrumbs
1 medium onion, peeled
½ teaspoon salt
2 tablespoons chopped fresh parsley
½ teaspoon lemon pepper
2 tablespoons lemon juice
oil for brushing
20 mini bamboo skewers, soaked in water for 30 minutes

Method

Place the chicken in a bowl. Add the breadcrumbs.

Using fine side of grater, grate the onion over the breadcrumbs to catch the juice. Add all remaining ingredients except the oil.

Mix and knead well with your hands to combine and make the chicken mix fine.

Stand for 15 minutes.

With wet hands take a portion of chicken and mould around the stick to a 35 mm length.

Arrange on an oiled tray, cover and refrigerate for 1 hour.

Prepare the barbecue for medium–hot direct-heat cooking.

Oil the grill and place the chicken sticks on.

Cook for 10–12 minutes, or until cooked through, turning frequently.

Serve hot.

Tandoori Chicken Legs

Serves 4

Ingredients

250 g (9 fl oz) plain yoghurt
1 garlic clove, crushed
1 chilli, finely chopped
1½ teaspoons cumin
1 teaspoon ground coriander
1 teaspoon cinnamon
1 teaspoon paprika
1 teaspoon fresh ginger
1 tablespoon tomato paste
1 lemon, cut into wedges
10 x chicken legs
2 teaspoons garam masala
¼ bunch coriander, roughly chopped

Method

Place the yoghurt, garlic, chilli, cumin, ground coriander, cinnamon, paprika, fresh ginger, tomato paste and juice from half of the lemon in a large bowl and combine well.

Prepare the chicken, making two slits; one on each side of the drumsticks 1 cm deep. Place the drumsticks in a large bowl.

Add the yoghurt mixture and turn to coat well. Cover and refrigerate for at least 3 hours, overnight if possible.

Cook the drumsticks on a lightly oiled medium–high heat barbecue grill for 30–40 minutes, depending on the size of your drumsticks. Close the barbecue hood but continue to turn the drumsticks every 5 minutes.

Grill the chicken until no longer pink when cut close to the bone and the juices run clear. Reduce the heat if needed to ensure the drumsticks don't overcook or burn.

Serve the drumsticks on a large platter, lightly sprinkled with garam masala and garnished with coriander and lemon wedges.

Chicken Skewers

Serves 4–6

Ingredients

500 g (18 oz) chicken breast or thigh fillets
2 tablespoons soy sauce
2 tablespoons lemon juice
½ teaspoon sugar
clove garlic, crushed
1 tablespoon sweet chilli sauce
12 bamboo skewers, soaked in water for 30 minutes
1 cup plain yogurt
½ cup fresh mint leaves, chopped
1 clove small garlic, mince

Method

Cut the chicken into 2 cm (½ in) cubes. Mix the soy sauce, lemon juice, sugar, garlic and sweet chilli sauce to a smooth paste, adding a small amount of water if necessary to achieve a smooth consistency.

Add the chicken, mix well to cover with marinade and refrigerate for at least 30 minutes.

Meanwhile, soak 12 bamboo skewers in cold water.

To make the mint sauce mix together yogurt, mint leaves and crushed garlic refrigerate to ready to use.

Remove the chicken from the marinade and thread onto skewers.

Cook on the barbecue, brushing occasionally with leftover marinade, for 6–8 minutes or until chicken is cooked.

Sticky Beer Can Chicken

Serves 4

Ingredients

1 large whole chicken

1 teaspoon vegetable oil

¼ teaspoon pepper

½ teaspoon sea salt

½ teaspoon chicken spice rub

1 can beer (or soft drink can may also be used)

2 tablespoons barbecue sauce

Method

Pat down the chicken with a paper towel to absorb any moisture.

Rub the chicken inside and out with vegetable oil. Season with salt, pepper and spice rub.

Open the beer can and pour out ½ of the liquid. Place the can on a cutting board and lower the chicken on to the can so it looks like it is sitting on it. Position the legs like a tripod so the chicken sits upright.

Prepare the barbecue for indirect cooking.

Place the chicken in the middle of the barbecue and close lid.

Cook the chicken for about a 1 hour or until golden brown.

The chicken is done when the juices run clear when skewer is pushed into thickest part of the thigh.

Brush the chicken with barbecue sauce and cook for a further 10 minutes until dark and sticky.

Jerk Chicken

Serves 4

Ingredients

8 pieces chicken Maryland (drumstick and thigh, bone in)
1 bunch spring onions (scallions)
2 cloves of garlic
1 jalapeño chilli
45 ml (1½ fl oz) fresh lime juice
45 ml (1½ fl oz) olive oil
4 teaspoons brown sugar
1½ teaspoons ground allspice
1 teaspoon dried thyme
½ teaspoon ground cinnamon
coarse salt, to taste

Method

Marinade: in a blender, combine spring onions, garlic, jalapeño, lime juice, oil, sugar, allspice, thyme, cinnamon, 1 teaspoon of salt and 45 ml (1½ fl oz) olive oil. Blend until smooth. Set aside 60 ml (2 fl oz) for brushing.

Place chicken in a shallow dish; season all over with salt.

Pour remaining marinade over chicken and toss to coat.

Cover and refrigerate, turning once or twice, for at least two hours (up to overnight).

Heat grill to medium high. Oil grates.

Lift chicken from marinade and let excess drip off. Place on grill and cover.

Cook, turning occasionally, until chicken is blackened in spots (about 10 minutes).

Move chicken to a cooler part of the grill and brush with reserved marinade.

Grill, covered, until chicken is cooked through (10–15 minutes more).

Serve immediately.

Cajun Chicken

Serves 4

Ingredients

4 chicken breasts on the bone, skin on
20 ml (⅔ fl oz) olive oil
8 teaspoons Cajun spice
20 ml (⅔ fl oz) barbecue sauce or HP sauce.
120 ml (4 fl oz) tomato and chilli pickle
2 sprigs fresh oregano

Method

Rinse the chicken, pat well to dry if necessary, and smooth the skin over the breast.

Rub the chicken all over with oil, then rub the Cajun spices over with your fingers, massaging them in.

Place the chicken breasts in a deep container, skin side up.

Cover with a lid or wrap that does not touch the top of the chicken.

Refrigerate for 2 hours or more, or just stand at room temperature for 20 minutes, then cook. Longer marinating time enhances the taste.

Prepare the barbecue for indirect-heat cooking and insert a drip tray. Heat to medium.

Place the chicken breasts, skin side up, onto the oiled grill over the drip tray. Close the lid or hood and cook for 40 minutes; no need to turn.

During the final cooking, open the lid and brush lightly with barbecue sauce a few times to glaze. The chicken is cooked when the juices run clear when pricked with a skewer. Remove from the grill and keep hot.

Place a spoonful of pickle on top of each chicken breast and garnish with half a sprig of fresh oregano.

Tasty Chicken Wings

Serves 6–8

Ingredients

2 kg (approx. 4½ lb) chicken wings
300 ml (10 fl oz) honey
juice of 1 orange
4 teaspoons fresh parsley, finely chopped
4 teaspoons fresh oregano, finely chopped
1 teaspoon allspice
2 teaspoons soy sauce
2 limes, sliced into thin circles
2 spring onions (scallions), diagonally sliced

Method

Place the wings in a large stainless steel baking dish. Combine the honey, orange juice, herbs, soy sauce and allspice to form a marinade and pour over the wings.

Coat both sides. Cover and marinate in refrigerator for at least 4 hours or, preferably, overnight.

Prepare the limes and spring onions and take with the chicken to the barbecue area.

Prepare the barbecue for indirect-heat cooking and heat to medium.

Add 120 ml (4 fl oz) of water to the wings in the dish.

Turn and mix through, then spread wings to a single layer.

Cover with a lid, and place over indirect heat for 45–50 minutes.

Turn the wings occasionally.

Lift the wings with tongs and place on well-oiled grill bars over direct heat for 1–2 minutes on each side to crisp.

Place the lime slices on the grill for 1 minute each side, brushing with a little marinade.

Remove the chicken wings to a platter, garnish with lime slices and sprinkle with the spring onions.

Chicken Wingette Pops

Serves 4

Ingredients

10 chicken wingettes (the two-bone bit, not the little drumstick)
1 tablespoon soy sauce
½ teaspoon chilli powder
½ teaspoon cracked
black pepper
125 ml (5 oz) polenta
250 ml (9 fl oz) vegetable or canola oil
2 tablespoons sriracha sauce
3 tablespoons mayonnaise

Method

Cut the wings into drumettes and the wingette pieces.

For each chicken wing, push the meat down to one end and remove the thin bone. Leave the thick bone and pull the meat past the end, creating the 'lollypop'.

Combine the soy sauce, chilli and black pepper to make a marinade.

Place the chicken pops in the marinade for 30 minutes.

Dry each chicken pop on paper towel.

Place the polenta in a shallow bowl and coat each chicken pop in the polenta.

Heat the oil in a frying pan until hot on the grill of the barbecue directly (when a wooden skewer bubbles when placed in the oil).

Shallow-fry the chicken pops for 3–4 minutes on each side, or until golden brown.

Combine the sriracha sauce and mayonnaise in a small serving bowl.

Serve the chicken pops with the sriracha mayonnaise.

Grilled Chicken with Orange

Serves 4–6

Ingredients

55 g (2 oz) butter
6 chicken joints, breasts, thighs or Marylands (thigh and drumsticks)
1 lemon, cut in half
salt, to taste
1 large orange, thinly sliced

Method

Melt the butter in a small pan. Rub the chicken with half of the cut lemon, brush it liberally with melted butter and sprinkle lightly with salt.

Prepare the barbecue to medium–hot. Place the chicken, inner side up, on the grill about10 cm above the heat.

Cook for 10–12 minutes then turn it skin side up and cook for a further 10–15 minutes, brushing with butter several times during cooking.

The chicken is ready when the skin is crisp and golden and the juices run colourless when the thickest part of the flesh is pierced with a skewer.

To make the dressing, squeeze the juice from the other half of the lemon into the rest of the butter – add a little more butter if necessary.

Pile the pea shoots on a platter or individual plates.

Serve the chicken on top with the dressing poured over.

Garnish with the orange slices.

Sticky Orange Chicken Wings

Serves 4–6

Ingredients

12 chicken wings
300 ml (12 fl oz) bottle hoisin or barbecue sauce
3 oranges
4 green salad leaves
3 spring onions, sliced

Method

Place the chicken wings in a shallow non-metallic dish and pour over the sauce. Squeeze the juice from 1 orange and pour into the empty sauce bottle.

Give it a shake to release all the remaining sauce, then pour the juice over the chicken.

Turn the chicken to coat well, cover and place in the refrigerator to marinate for 10 minutes.

Prepare the barbecue for direct high heat.

Place the chicken wings in a single layer on the grill for 20 minutes, turning frequently and basting with the sauce, until the flesh is cooked through and the skin is charred.

Meanwhile, peel the remaining oranges and divide into segments.

Divide the salad leaves between 4 plates, add the orange segments and spring onions and top with the hot chicken wings.

Mini Drum Sticks

Serves 4

Ingredients

1 kg (2¼ lb) chicken wings
tablespoon salt
½ teaspoon pepper

Method

Cut your chicken wings into drumettes and wingettes and discard the tips or use to make chicken stock.

Put the wings in a large freezer bag and the salt and pepper to season.

Prepare your barbecue for direct heat cooking on the grill at a medium high heat cook until golden brown, crispy and completely cooked through, around 20 minutes.

If you have any flare-ups or the wings begin to burn, move the wings to a cooler part of the grill or reduce the heat.

Put on a platter and serve with your favourite sauces.

Quick Sesame Chicken Wings

Serves 4–6

Ingredients

2 kg (4½ lb) chicken wings, tips removed
½ cup honey
3 tablespoons light soy sauce
2 tablespoons sherry
½ teaspoon fresh ginger, minced
½ teaspoon fresh garlic, minced
3 tablespoons sesame seeds, toasted
spring onion or parsley finely sliced, to serve

Method

Combine the honey, soy sauce, sherry, ginger and garlic together. Stir together to make a marinade.

Place the wings in a large container. Cover with marinade and place in the refrigerator for 1 hour.

Place half the wings in a microwave-safe dish and microwave for 7 minutes on high.

Remove and microwave the remainder.

Heat the barbecue until hot. Place a wire cake-rack over the grill bars and place the wings on the rack.

Brush with any marinade left in the bowl.

Turn and brush the wings frequently for 6 minutes until brown and crisp.

While the wings are crisping, spread the sesame seeds on a foil tray and place on the barbecue. Shake occasionally as they toast.

Sprinkle sesame seeds and spring onion over the chicken wings and serve.

Sticky Chicken Drumettes

Serves 4–6

Ingredients

1 kg (2¼ lb) chicken drumettes
3 tablespoons soy sauce
3 tablespoons barbecue sauce
3 tablespoons honey
1 garlic clove, crushed
1 teaspoon salt
½ teaspoon pepper

Method

Place the drumettes in a large freezer bag. Add the remaining ingredients and shake the bag to coat the drumettes. Refrigerate until needed.

Preheat the barbecue grill to medium–high heat. Cook the drumettes for 15–20 minutes, or until golden brown, crispy and completely cooked through.

Keep basting the chicken with the marinade throughout the cooking process.

If the drumettes begin to burn, move the wings to a cooler part of the grill or reduce the heat.

Remove from the barbecue and place on a platter to serve.

Barbecued Chicken and Avocado Quesadilla

Serves 2

Ingredients

2 chicken breasts
1 red onion, finely sliced
1 garlic clove, finely sliced
1 avocado, cut into long, thin slices
100 g (3½ oz) cheddar cheese
100 g (3½ oz) provolone cheese
8 flour tortillas
4 tablespoons barbecue rub

Method

Rub the chicken with combined spices until coated evenly and leave to stand for 30 minutes.

Lightly fry the onion and garlic on an oiled barbecue flatplate until golden. Remove and set aside until needed.

Add the lightly oiled chicken fillet and grill for 4–5 minutes per side (depending on thickness of the fillets), or until cooked through.

Remove the chicken from the barbecue, place on a cutting board and cut into 1 cm slices.

Place the chicken, avocado, onion, garlic and cheeses onto the flour tortillas.

Cover with a tortilla.

Place on the barbecue flatplate until lightly toasted on both sides and the cheese is melted.

Cut and serve warm.

Tandoori Chicken Legs

Serves 4–6

Ingredients

10 x chicken legs
240 g (8 oz) plain yoghurt
1 garlic clove, crushed
1 chilli, finely chopped
1½ teaspoons cumin
1 teaspoon ground coriander (cilantro)
1 teaspoon cinnamon
1 teaspoon paprika
1 teaspoon fresh ginger
20 ml (⅔ fl oz) tomato paste
1 lemon, cut into wedges
2 teaspoons garam masala
¼ bunch coriander (cilantro), roughly chopped

Method

Place the yoghurt, garlic, chilli, cumin, ground coriander, cinnamon, paprika, fresh ginger, tomato paste and juice from half of the lemon in a large bowl and combine well.

Prepare the chicken, making two slits; one on each side of the drumsticks 1 cm (2/5 in) deep. Place in a large bowl.

Add the yoghurt mixture and turn to coat well. Cover and refrigerate for at least 3 hours, overnight if possible. Cook the drumsticks on a lightly oiled medium–high heat barbecue grill for 30–40 minutes, depending on the size of your drumsticks. Close the barbecue hood but continue to turn the drumsticks every 5 minutes.

Grill the chicken until no longer pink when cut close to the bone and the juices run clear. Reduce the heat if needed to ensure the drumsticks don't overcook or burn.

Serve the drumsticks on a large platter, lightly sprinkled with garam masala and garnished with coriander (cilantro) and lemon wedges.

Chicken and Vegetable Skewers

Serves 4

Ingredients

4 chicken breast fillets, cut into 2.5 cm (1 in) cubes
210 g (7 oz) button mushrooms
3 onions, cut in quarters
2 yellow capsicum (peppers), cut in to 2 cm pieces
1 x 225 g (7 ½ oz) can pineapple rings, cut into wedges
1 large lemon, cut into thin slices

Marinade

juice and zest of 1 lemon
1 teaspoon garlic powder
1 teaspoon lemon pepper
salt and pepper, to taste
½ bunch flat-leaf parsley, roughly chopped

Method

Soak the skewers for 20 minutes (if using bamboo skewers).

Place chicken, mushroom, onion, capsicum, pineapple on skewer and then fold a lemon slice and add. Continue until the skewer is full.

Place the skewers in a deep-sided dish or tray.

Combine the marinade ingredients and coat the skewers.

Leave to marinate for 15 minutes.

Cook the skewers on a medium–high barbecue grill, turning every 2–3 minutes or until cooked through.

Serve with a fresh leaf salad, if you like.

Tandoori Chicken Pieces

Serves 4

Ingredients

6 chicken Maryland pieces, skin off
salt
200ml (7 fl oz) natural yoghurt
tandoori paste, to taste
1 tablespoon butter or ghee, melted
crisp lettuce leaves
1 lemon
1 packet flatbread (Lebanese bread)

Method

Prick the meat all over with a skewer. Sprinkle lightly with salt.

Mix the yogurt with 4 tablespoons of the tandoori paste, adding more to taste if desired. With fingers, rub mixture all over the chicken pieces, rubbing well into the slashes. Place into a non-metallic dish, cover and marinate in refrigerator for 6 hours or overnight.

Place chicken on a greased baking tray.

Pour the excess marinade from the dish into a bowl. Stir butter or ghee into the marinade. Transfer all to the barbecue area.

Prepare the barbecue for indirect-heat cooking. Set up a drip pan with a cup of water in the pan.

Place the chicken on the well-oiled grill bars over the drip pan.

Cover and cook for 40 minutes or until cooked. Brush with the reserved marinade at 10 minute intervals for first half of cooking, then at 5 minute intervals.

At the last 5 minutes, place flatbreads into barbecue to heat over direct heat.

Remove from grill. Place on a platter lined with lettuce leaves.

Garnish with lemon slices.

Cut each flatbread into 6 triangular pieces and serve with the tandoori chicken.

Chicken Skewers

Serves 6–12

Ingredients

500 g (18 oz) chicken breast or thigh fillets
2 tablespoons soy sauce
2 tablespoons lemon juice
½ teaspoon sugar
clove garlic, crushed
1 tablespoon sweet chilli sauce
12 bamboo skewers, soaked in water for 30 minutes
1 cup plain yogurt
½ cup fresh mint leaves, chopped
1 clove small garlic, mince

Method

Cut the chicken into 2 cm (1 in) cubes.

Mix the soy sauce, lemon juice, sugar, garlic and sweet chilli sauce to a smooth paste, adding a small amount of water if necessary to achieve a smooth consistency.

Add the chicken, mix well to cover with marinade and refrigerate for at least 30 minutes.

Meanwhile, soak 12 bamboo skewers in cold water. To make the mint sauce mix together yogurt, mint leaves and crushed garlic refrigerate to ready to use.

Remove the chicken from the marinade and thread onto skewers.

Cook on the barbecue, brushing occasionally with leftover marinade, for 6–8 minutes or until chicken is cooked.

Somebody once told me that mint was a stimulant and that it helps your body to consume fat rather than store it! I would like to pretend that serving these skewers with a beautiful mint sauce is part of my weight management regime but the truth is much simpler than that – the taste of chicken and mint together is sensational!

SEAFOOD

Barbecue Oysters with Parmesan Butter

Serves 4

Ingredients

12 large oysters, shucked
100 g (3½ oz) parmesan butter
rock salt, to taste
lemon wedges, to serve
Tabasco sauce, to serve

Method

Place 1 teaspoon of butter onto each oyster.

Place the oysters on a hot barbecue grill and close the lid for 2–3 minutes until the butter melts.

Leave to cool slightly as the shells will be hot.

Place on a serving platter scattered with rock salt to seat the oyster (so you don't lose the butter).

Serve with a few wedges of lemon and hot sauce such as Tabasco.

Parmesan, Garlic and Parsley Butter

Serves 4

Ingredients

100 g (3½ oz) softened butter
3 tablespoons finely grated parmesan cheese
1 garlic clove, crushed
2 tablespoons chopped
flat-leaf parsley
salt and pepper, to taste

Method

Mix the ingredients in a bowl until smooth.

Place the mixture onto a piece of plastic wrap and roll into a tube shape, twisting the ends and tie.

Place in the freezer until firm, then cut into slices just before use.

Barbecued Oysters in Chilli Sauce

Serves 4

Ingredients

12 oysters in the half shell
1 tablespoon unsalted butter
½ teaspoon crushed garlic
2 tablespoons lemon juice
2 tablespoons chilli sauce
pared lemon zest to garnish
chilli flakes to garnish

Method

In a small pan, melt the butter, add the garlic and cook just until the butter colours.

Remove from heat, add the lemon juice and chilli sauce, stir to combine.

Prepare a metal tray (e.g. Swiss roll tin) with a layer of cooking salt about 1 cm deep. Transport sauce, tray and oysters to the barbecue.

Place the tray of salt on grill over direct high heat.

When salt has heated well, remove to the side.

Place the oysters in the tin, pushing shells into the salt to prevent them tipping.

With a teaspoon spoon sauce over each oyster.

Replace the tray on the grill and cook for 5–6 minutes or until sauce around the oyster bubbles.

Remove immediately and serve garnished with lemon zest and chilli flakes.

For larger quantities of oysters adjust sauce quantity per 6 or 12 oysters.

Angels on Horseback

Serves 4

Ingredients

12 large oysters, freshly shucked or from a bottle
6 streaky bacon strips
lemon wedges, to serve

Method

Cut each slice of bacon in half and wrap the oysters in bacon. Overlap the ends, securing with a toothpick or short skewer.

On hot grill, cook until the bacon is crisp (depending on the thickness of your bacon).

Serve while warm with a wedge of lemon.

Soak the toothpicks or skewers in water for 20–30 minutes.

Oysters in White Wine

Serves 10–12

Ingredients

48 freshly shucked small Pacific oysters, in the shell
1 cup white wine
2 tablespoons chives, chopped
1 teaspoon pink peppercorns, rinsed and roughly crushed
250 g (9 oz) salted butter, in 2 cm (1 in) cubes

Method

Check the oysters are grit free – but try not to rinse under running water as you will lose that saltwater flavour of freshly shucked oysters.

Boil the wine and simmer for 2 minutes; add the chives and peppercorns and simmer for a further minute.

Remove from the heat and swirl in the butter to melt and combine well.

Put the oysters, onto the open barbecue grill.

Spoon over some of the sauce.

When the liquid is bubbling, the oysters are ready to serve.

Lift the oysters from the barbecue and place them onto heaped rock salt on a platter to keep the oysters upright, or on finely shredded outer lettuce leaves for the same purpose.

Leave to cool so they can be picked up and easily slipped out of the shell.

Grilled Oysters with Champagne

Serves 4

Ingredients

12 fresh oysters in their shells, pre-shucked
½ cup fish stock
¼ cup Champagne
30 g (1 oz) butter
2 tablespoons thickened cream
freshly ground black pepper
50 g (1¾ oz) baby spinach

Method

Combination Cooktop and Grill

Place the oyster shells in a flameproof dish lined with crumpled foil so that the shells sit level.

Bring the fish stock to a simmer and poach the oysters for 30–60 seconds, until just firm.

Remove oysters from the pan, add the Champagne and boil for 2 minutes to reduce.

Remove from the heat and whisk in the butter, then the cream.

Season with pepper.

Preheat the grill to high. Cook the spinach in a saucepan of water for 2–3 minutes until wilted. Squeeze out the excess liquid and divide between the shells.

Top with an oyster and spoon over a little sauce.

Cook close to the grill for 1 minute or until heated through.

Barbecued Oysters in Chilli Sauce

Serves 4

Ingredients

12 oysters in the half shell
1 tablespoon unsalted butter
½ teaspoon crushed garlic
2 tablespoons lemon juice
2 tablespoons chilli sauce
pared lemon zest to garnish
chilli flakes to garnish

Method

In a small pan, melt the butter, add the garlic and cook just until the butter colours.

Remove from heat, add the lemon juice and chilli sauce, stir to combine.

Prepare a metal tray (e.g. Swiss roll tin) with a layer of cooking salt about 1 cm deep. Transport sauce, tray and oysters to the barbecue.

Place the tray of salt on grill over direct high heat.

When salt has heated well, remove to the side.

Place the oysters in the tin, pushing shells into the salt to prevent them tipping.

With a teaspoon spoon sauce over each oyster.

Replace the tray on the grill and cook for 5–6 minutes or until sauce around the oyster bubbles.

Remove immediately and serve garnished with lemon zest and chilli flakes.

For larger quantities of oysters adjust sauce quantity per 6 or 12 oysters.

Barbecued Mussels with Chilli Lime Dressing

Serves 6–8

Ingredients

about 50 fresh green-lipped mussels in the shell
fresh chives or parsley for garnish

Chilli Lime Dressing

1 clove garlic, crushed and finely chopped
¼ cup fresh lime juice
1 tablespoon Thai fish sauce
½ teaspoon prepared minced chilli
½ teaspoon brown sugar

Method

Debeard the mussels.

Preheat the barbecue hotplate and place the muscles on top.

Cook until the mussels open, covering if you have a lidded barbecue.

Discard any mussels that do not open.

Break off and discard the top shell of the cooked mussels.

For the chilli lime dressing, mix the garlic, lime juice, fish sauce, chilli and brown sugar together.

Arrange the mussels on a platter and drizzle the dressing over them.

Garnish with chives.

As mussels die quickly after debearding, prepare them immediately before cooking.

Belgian-style Mussels

Serves 2–4

Ingredients

2 kg (4 lb 6 oz) mussels in their shells
30 g (1 oz) butter
1 tablespoon vegetable oil
4 French shallots, chopped
2 stalks celery, chopped, plus any leaves
⅔ cup dry white wine
freshly ground black pepper
½ cup thickened cream
½ cup fresh flat-leaf parsley, chopped

Method

Scrub the mussels under cold running water, then pull away any beards and discard any mussels that are open or damaged.

Heat grill on barbecue to medium.

Heat the butter and oil in a very large ironcast saucepan, then add the shallots or onion and celery and cook for 2–3 minutes until the shallots are translucent.

Stir in the wine and plenty of pepper and bring to the boil.

Add the mussels, cover and cook over a high heat, shaking the pan occasionally, for 4–5 minutes until the mussels have opened.

Remove from the pan and keep warm in a bowl, discarding any that remain closed. Roughly chop the celery leaves, reserving a few for garnish.

Add the chopped leaves, cream and parsley to the cooking juices and season again if necessary.

Bring to the boil on the grill of the barbecue, then spoon over the mussels.

Garnish with celery leaves.

Prawn (Shrimp) and Chorizo Skewers

Serves 4–6

Ingredients

1 kg (2¼ lb) green prawns/shrimp, peeled, tails on
3 chorizo sausages, cut into 1 cm pieces
coriander, to garnish
1 lemon, to serve

Prawn Marinade

1 red chilli, finely sliced
1 garlic clove
3 tablespoons olive oil
juice of 1 lemon
¼ teaspoon salt
½ tablespoon pepper

Method

To make the prawn marinade, combine all of the ingredients.

Marinate the prawns for 10 minutes.

Soak skewers for 20 minutes, if you're using bamboo skewers, before threading the prawns and chorizo alternately on the skewers.

Cook the skewers on a medium–high grill for 2–3 minutes on each side.

Squeeze the lemon on the skewers then garnish with coriander and serve warm.

Barbecue Teriyaki Tuna Skewers

Serves 4

Ingredients

4 tuna steaks, cut into 3 cm (1 in) cubes
sweet coleslaw, to serve optional

Marinade

4 tablespoons olive oil
1 teaspoon chilli flakes
1 teaspoon brown sugar
1 lime or lemon juice and zest (whichever you prefer)
¼ teaspoon black pepper

Method

To make the marinade, combine all of the ingredients.

Marinate the tuna in the marinade for 10 minutes.

Place the tuna on short skewers (soak the skewers for 20 minutes if using bamboo).

Preheat the barbecue grill to a medium–high heat.

Place the skewers on the grill and baste with the leftover marinade to keep moist.

Turn every 3–5 minutes. Cook until done to your liking.

Serve with sweet coleslaw or red Asian slaw and grilled asparagus.

Prawn (Shrimp) Skewers

Serves 4

Ingredients

36 green prawns/shrimp, peeled and deveined (tails on)
1½ tablespoons vegetable oil
2 tablespoons fish sauce
1 large red chilli, chopped and seeds removed
1 tablespoon palm sugar
2–3 cloves garlic, crushed
juice of 1 lime
8–10 bamboo skewers, soaked in water for 30 minutes

Lime Mayonnaise

2 egg yolks
1 cup olive oil
ground pepper
juice of 1 lime
¼ cup Coriander chopped

Method

Soak 12 bamboo skewers in cold water for at least 30 minutes.

Combine the vegetable oil, fish sauce, lime juice, fresh chilli, palm sugar and garlic in a large bowl.

Add the prawns, toss to coat in the mixture, cover and leave to marinate in the fridge for no more than 30 minutes.

In a food processor place the egg yolks and process until just combined. With machine running, gradually pour in oil and process until mixture thickens.

Blend in lime juice and pepper to taste. Be careful not to over process.

Add chopped coriander just before serving Prepare the barbecue for direct cooking.

Thread the prawns onto the skewers before grilling the prawns for 2 minutes on each side, or until just cooked.

Prosciutto Prawns/Shrimp

Serves 6–8

Ingredients

24 large green king prawns/shrimp, with middle section peeled and de-veined
24 bamboo skewers, soaked in water for 30 minutes, or metal skewers
12–24 slices prosciutto (this depends on how long each slice is)

Rocket Aïoli

4 medium cloves garlic
½ teaspoon sea salt
2 egg yolks
½ teaspoon lemon juice
½ cup blanched and well drained rocket
125 ml (5 fl oz) olive oil

Method

Take each prawn and thread it onto a skewer starting from the tail. Roll each prawn in prosciutto so as to cover all the prawn. The size of the slice of prosciutto will depend on the size of the prawns being used.

Store on a covered plate in the refrigerator until ready to use.

Cook the prawns on a medium–hot flat barbecue plate, turning regularly for even cooking.

When the top (head end) of the prawns are completely white, they are ready to eat. The prosciutto wraps around the prawn very tightly as it cooks.

For the rocket aïoli put the garlic, salt, egg yolks, lemon juice and rocket into the food processor and blend for 30 seconds.

When this mixture is starting to thicken, slowly pour the oil down the feeder shoot. As it takes, you can add the oil a little more quickly until finished.

Use immediately or store for up to five days.

Serve the prawns ready to dip in pots of the aïoli.

Spicy Barbecued Baby Octopus

Serves 4

Ingredients

1 kg (2¼ lb) baby octopus
400 ml (16 fl oz) red wine
100 ml (3½ fl oz) balsamic vinegar
1 garlic clove, crushed
50 ml (2 fl oz) soy sauce
50 ml (2 fl oz) hot sauce
50 ml (2 fl oz) barbecue sauce
50 ml (2 fl oz) tomato sauce
salt and pepper, to taste
20 g (¾ oz) chopped fresh coriander, to garnish
1 lemon, cut into wedges

Method

Place the octopus, red wine and balsamic vinegar in a saucepan and bring to the boil over medium heat.

Reduce to a simmer for 15 minutes.

Drain the octopus, then place in a large bowl.

Combine the garlic, soy sauce, hot sauce, tomato sauce and barbecue sauce.

Add to the octopus and mix to ensure the octopus is well coated.

Cook the octopus on a hot barbecue grill side, while basting with the sauce, for about 5 minutes or until charred. Do not over cook or they will be chewy.

When cooked, place on a serving plate with lemon and garnish with coriander.

Fish Tacos

Serves 4–8

Ingredients

1 egg
100 g (3½ oz) plain flour
½ teaspoon salt
1 teaspoon pepper
4 fillets of any firm flesh fish (such as snapper)
3 tablespoons olive oil
1 tablespoon butter
six 15 cm (6 in) soft tacos
sweet coleslaw if desired
coriander leaves, to garnish

Method

Whisk the egg. Combine the flour, salt and pepper.

Dip the fish fillets in the egg wash, then coat the fillets in the flour mix.

Place the fish fillets on a medium–high heat barbecue flatplate with the oil and butter.

Cook for 3–4 minutes on each side, or until golden brown.

Cut the fillets into long strips and place on the tacos with the sweet coleslaw. Garnish with coriander.

Bacon-wrapped Scallops with Spicy Mayo

Serves 4–6

Ingredients

12 streaky bacon strips
12 large sea scallops
½ teaspoon garlic powder
salt and pepper, to taste
lemon wedges, to serve

Spicy Mayo

60 g (2¼ fl oz) mayonnaise
2 tablespoons tomato sauce
1 tablespoon hot sauce
2 lemons (juice of half a lemon for the sauce and half to squeeze on before cooking)

Method

Cook the bacon on a barbecue flatplate so it is about half cooked through, then leave to cool.

Wrap each scallop with a slice of bacon and secure it with a toothpick or short skewer. Squeeze over the lemon and garlic powder, then season with salt and pepper.

Cook the bacon on a hot barbecue grill until it is sizzling and the scallops are opaque.

Meanwhile, make the spicy seafood sauce.

Mix together the mayonnaise, tomato sauce, hot sauce and lemon juice in a bowl. Refrigerate until needed.

Serve the scallops while still warm with lemon wedges and spicy mayo.

Fish Kebabs

Serves 4

Ingredients

800 g (1¾ lb) fish, cubed
bamboo skewers (pre-soaked in water)
chopped parsley

Marinade

2 cloves garlic, finely chopped
1 small red chilli, finely chopped
pinch sea salt
½ lemon, juiced
240 ml (8 fl oz) olive oil

Method

Thread fish cubes onto skewers.

Combine all marinade ingredients.

Place kebabs in a baking dish and cover with marinade.

Refrigerate, turning occasionally, for 15 minutes.

Heat barbecue to medium high. Cook on a barbecue plate or in a baking dish or grill for approximately 10 to 15 minutes depending on the type of fish you use, until fish is cooked.

Add parsley to garnish.

Preparing Fish

The two types of fish discussed here are described as flatfish (for example, flounder or sole) and round fish (for example, snapper or cod).

Both types need to be cleaned before use, but cleaning procedures vary.

SCALING AND FINNING

Most fish will need to be scaled. However, there are a few exceptions, such as trout, tuna, shark, leatherjacket and others. When poaching a whole unboned fish, it is best to leave the dorsal and anal fins attached.

This will help to hold the fish together during cooking.

Wash fish and leave wet, as a wet fish is easier to scale.

Remove scales using a knife or scaler, starting at the tail and scraping towards the head

Clip the dorsal fin with scissors or, if desired, remove both the dorsal and anal fins by cutting along the side of the fin with a sharp knife. Then pull the fin towards the head to remove it

GUTTING

Gutting techniques are different for round fish and flatfish.

When preparing fish to bone or fillet, remove the entrails by gutting through the belly. If you wish to serve the fish whole, preserve the shape of the fish by gutting through the gills.

Round Fish

For boning or filleting, cut off the head behind the gill opening. Use a sharp knife and cut open the belly from head to just above anal fin. Remove membranes, veins and viscera. Rinse thoroughly.

To preserve shape of round fish, cut through the gills and open outer gill with the thumb. Put a finger into the gill and snag the inner gill. Gently pull to remove inner gill and viscera. Rinse well.

Flatfish

To gut, make a small cut behind gills and pull out viscera.

SKINNING

The tasty skin of some fish enhances the flavour. However, other fish have strong or inedible skin that interferes with the flavour. Always leave skin on when poaching or grilling a whole fish.

Round fish

When skinning a whole round fish, make a slit across the body behind the gills, with another just above the tail. Then make another cut down the back.

Using a sharp knife, start at the tail and separate the skin from the flesh. Pull the knife towards the head, while holding the skin firmly with the other hand – do not use a sawing motion.

Flatfish

To skin a whole flatfish, first turn the dark side up, then cut across the skin where the tail joins the body . With a sharp knife, peel the skin back towards the head until you have enough skin to hold with one hand.

Anchor the fish with one hand and pull the skin over the head. Turn fish over and hold the head while pulling the skin down to the tail.

CUTTING FILLETS

Fillets are pieces of boneless fish. There are slightly different techniques for filleting round fish and flatfish.

Round fish

With a sharp knife, make a slit along the backbone from head to tail, then make a cut behind the gills. Hold the head and insert the knife between fillet and ribs. Slide knife along the ribs (do not use a sawing motion), and cut down the length of the fish. Remove fillet by cutting off at the anal fin. Repeat on the other side of fish.

Flatfish

Place skinned fish on chopping board with eyes up. Cut from head to tail through the flesh to the backbone, down the middle of the fish. Insert a sharp knife between the ribs and the end of the fillet near the head. Pull knife down the fillet on one side of the backbone and remove.

Cut off the remaining fillet in the same manner. Turn fish over and remove the two bottom fillets.

SKINNING A FILLET

Place fillet skin-side down and cut a small piece of flesh away from the skin close to the tail. Hold skin tight, and run a sharp knife along the skin without cutting it.

CUTTING A STEAK OR CUTLET

Using a solid, sharp chef's knife, cut off head just behind the gills. Slice the fish into steaks or cutlets of the desired thickness.

CLEANING PRAWNS/SHRIMP

Most people prefer to remove the head and body shell before eating. However, the entire body of the prawn/shrimp is edible, depending on the cooking method. To peel, break off head, place finger on underside between legs, and roll prawn. The body shell will come away. Then squeeze tail section, and remainder of shell will slip off.

Slit down the middle of the outside curve to expose the intestinal vein.

Remove it, and wash prawn under cold, running water. It is not necessary to remove the vein from bay or smaller prawns. However, veins of larger prawns sometimes contain shell or grit that can affect taste.

CLEANING OCTOPUS

Cut head from body section, just below the eyes, to remove tentacles. Cut out eyes and clean body cavity. Push beak up through centre of joined tentacles, cut off and dispose. Wash thoroughly. Pay particular attention to tentacles as the suckers may contain sand.

Skin is difficult to remove from fresh octopus, but it may be left on for cooking.

However, to remove skin, parboil in a little water for 5–10 minutes, then skin when cool enough to handle. To clean a small, whole octopus, cut up back of head and remove gut. Push beak up and cut out. Cut out eyes and wash thoroughly.

CLEANING LOBSTER

You can purchase whole live or frozen lobster. Also available are uncooked frozen lobster tails and canned or frozen lobster meat.

To kill a live lobster, hold it on its back on a firm surface. With a heavy chef's knife, stab the point into the mouth to sever the spinal cord.

You may also stun the lobster by placing it in the freezer for 30 minutes per 500 g (18 oz).

Weigh to calculate cooking time. Place live lobster in a large pot of cold, salty water and bring to simmering point. Simmer, but do not boil, for 8 minutes per 500 g (18 oz).

Hold lobster right-side up on a firm surface. Pierce the shell at the centre of the body behind the head.

Cut lobster in half lengthwise, and remove and discard sac near the head and intestinal vein in the tail.

Remove any 'mustard' from the body and reserve for flavouring your sauces. Clean the lobster by rinsing under cold, running water.

OYSTERS

If you use technique rather than strength, oysters are easy to open.

Hold the unopened oyster in a garden glove or tea towel to protect your hand from the rough shell, and open the shell with an oyster knife held in the other hand.

Insert the tip of the oyster knife into the hinge (the pointed end), then twist to open the shell. Do not open oyster by attempting to insert the oyster knife into the front lip of the shell.

Slide the oyster knife inside the upper shell to cut the muscle that attaches oyster to the shell. To serve, discard the upper part of shell and cut muscle under bottom half, then replace oyster into half-shell.

THE KEY TO FRESH FISH

Don't buy fish that has already been frozen.

Fish should not have a strong odour – instead it should have a pleasant, sea smell.

Whole fish should have bright eyes and red gills.

The flesh should be firm, with slippery skin and no yellow discolouration.

Whole Snapper in Foil

Serves 2

Ingredients

1 medium snapper per two people
 – allow approximately 250–300 g (9–11 oz) of fish per person
½ teaspoon black cracked pepper
½ tablespoon fish sauce
1 tablespoon soy sauce
1 lime, sliced, plus extra to serve
1 lemongrass stem, cut in half
2–3 spring onions, finely chopped
1 small chilli, finely sliced
¼ bunch basil leaves, roughly chopped (reserve some for garnish)
¼ bunch coriander, roughly chopped (reserve some for garnish)
2–3 tablespoons olive oil
2 carrot, cut into matchsticks
1 celery stalk, cut into matchsticks
2 spring onions, finely chopped
125 ml (4½ fl oz) sesame oil
1 lime

See Method on next page

Method

Rinse the fish inside and out under running water.

Pat dry with paper towel. Make three cuts 2½ cm (¾ in) apart, roughly 1 cm (½ in) deep in thickest part of fish on each side.

Rub the pepper, fish sauce and soy sauce into both sides of the skin of the fish and place the lime slices, lemongrass stalk, spring onions, chilli, basil and coriander inside the cavity of the fish.

Drizzle both sides of the fish with olive oil.

Place a sheet of foil with a piece of baking paper roughly the size the fish in the middle (this will stop the skin sticking to the foil). Place the fish on the paper and foil. Cover the fish with another sheet of baking paper and foil then fold in the sides to enclose, ensuring the fish is well sealed.

Place the fish on the barbecue grill (medium heat) and close the lid for 10–15 minutes. Turn and cook for a further 10 minutes on the other side, depending on the size of your fish (may need longer if you barbecue doesn't have a lid).

Remove from the barbecue and carefully unwrap only the top layer. Test the fish is cooked using a fork, seeing if it flakes apart easily.

Place on a serving platter. Sprinkle the carrot, celery and spring onions over the fish. Heat the sesame oil until just smoking, then carefully pour the oil over the fish. Serve with the reserved coriander, basil and the lime slices.

Barbecued Whole Snapper

Serves 6

Ingredients

1 whole snapper, about 1½ kg (5 lb)
½ red capsicum, chopped
¼ cup fresh basil, chopped
2 tablespoons lemon juice
1 tablespoon olive oil

Gherkin mayonnaise

1 cup mayonnaise
1 cup gherkin relish or chopped gherkins

Method

Scale the fish and rinse well. Pat dry with paper towels. To make the gherkin mayonnaise, mix mayonnaise and gherkin relish or chopped gherkin together. Set aside.

Mix the capsicum, basil, lemon juice and oil together. Spoon some into the cavity and spread the remainder over the fish.

Lay the fish on a large sheet of oiled foil and roll up the edges to form an enclosure around the fish. Place on a wire cake rack and place the rack on top of the grill bars, elevating so the fish is 10 cm (4 in) above the source of heat. Cook for 10–12 minutes on each side. Turn carefully using a large spatula, or place the fish in a hinged fish rack and turn when needed.

Serve fish while hot.

Snapper, potato wedges and salad! The perfect combination for Sunday lunch in the height of summer. You probably wondering where gherkin mayonnaise fits in? But, trust me, take a little time to whip it up and the mayonnaise will take this meal to a new level.

Grilled Fish

Serves 4

Ingredients

4 flathead medium size or any firm white fish
2 tablespoons sumac spice
4 tablespoons olive oil
bunch of fresh dill
2 lemons
8–12 wooden skewers, soaked for 30 minutes

Method

Ask the fish monger to clean and gut the fish and remove the head. Cut off the fins and trim the tail with a pair of kitchen scissors.

In a small bowl mix together the olive oil and the sumac.

Slice the lemons. Wash the dill and trim off the stalks.

Place the fish on their backs on a chopping board.

Into each fish cavity place a good handful of dill and 2–3 slices of lemon, then pour on some of the oil and sumac mix.

With 2–3 small wooden skewers, fasten together the fish so the dill and lemon do not fall out during cooking.

Turn the fish over and rub the oil and sumac mix well into the fish.

Prepare the barbecue for direct-heat cooking. Oil the grill bars well.

Cook the fish on each side for 8–10 minutes.

Serve with mixed salad.

Scampi with Basil Butter

Serves 2–4

Ingredients

12 raw scampi or yabbies, heads removed

Basil Butter

90 g (3 oz) butter, melted
¼ cup fresh basil, chopped
1 clove garlic, crushed
2 teaspoons honey

Method

Cut scampi or yabbies in half lengthwise.

To make basil butter, place butter, basil, garlic and honey in a small bowl and whisk to combine.

Brush each cut side of scampi or yabbie with basil butter and cook under a preheated hot grill for 2 minutes or until they change colour and are tender.

Drizzle with any remaining basil butter and serve immediately.

Salmon Fillet with Asian Dressing

Serves 4

Ingredients

4 salmon fillets
2 carrots, cut into matchsticks
2 sticks of celery, cut into matchsticks
100 g (3½ oz) bean sprouts
2–3 spring onions, thinly sliced coriander, roughly chopped, to garnish

Dressing

1 garlic clove, crushed
1 tablespoon soy sauce
125 ml (4½ fl oz) rice vinegar
3 tablespoons caster sugar
125 ml (4½ fl oz) olive oil
½ teaspoon toasted sesame oil
½ teaspoon salt
1 teaspoon freshly ground pepper

Method

Combine all of the dressing ingredients and place in saucepan over medium heat. Stir until the caster sugar has dissolved and the mixture has thickened slightly. Allow to cool for 15 minutes.

Place the salmon fillets, skin side down, on a medium–high flatplate and cook for 3–4 minutes or until the skin is crispy. Turn the fillets over and cook until the salmon is cooked to your liking (about 2–3 minutes depending on the thickness of the fillets).

Combine the dressing and carrots, celery, beansprouts and spring onions.

Mound the vegetables and place a salmon fillet on top. Garnish with coriander.

Salmon Fillets

Serves 4

Ingredients

4 skinless salmon fillets
350 g (12 oz) jasmine rice
½ cup sesame seeds
2 tablespoons olive oil
1 cup Thai marinade store bought or make your own
1 bunch of spring onions

Method

Steam the rice, mix through the sesame seeds and place in a container suitable for reheating.

Rub the salmon with oil and pour over the Thai marinade, making sure it covers both sides of the fish. Cover and set aside for 20 minutes.

Cut the spring onions diagonally into 25 mm (1 in) lengths, including some of the green tops. Place onto 2 foil squares, pour over a little of the marinade and wrap into a parcel with a double fold top and sides. Take everything to the barbecue area.

Prepare the barbecue for direct-heat grilling and heat to hot. Place the steamed rice at edge of the grill to keep hot.

Oil the grill well. Place the salmon and the foil parcel of spring onions on the grill and cook for 2 minutes.

Turn the salmon and the foil parcel and cook for 2 minutes more. Remove the parcel.

Cook the salmon until done.

Divide the onions between 4 plates on top of a mound of rice and the Thai salmon.

Serve immediately.

Swordfish Steaks with Tomato Salsa

Serves 4

Ingredients

1 tablespoon olive oil
4 swordfish steaks, evenly sized
extra oil, for the chargrill

Tomato Salsa

2 Roma tomatoes, finely chopped
1 small red onion, finely chopped
1 teaspoon freshly ground black pepper
2 tablespoons chopped fresh basil
2 tablespoons extra virgin olive oil
½ avocado
1 tablespoon lemon juice

Method

Sprinkle olive oil over each swordfish steak and set aside.

Heat a chargrill and cook the fish for 2–3 minutes on each side.

Combine all the salsa ingredients in a small bowl, and mix well.

Serve the fish with salsa over the top. Add salt and pepper for extra taste.

Grill swordfish until the outside is browned but inside is still slightly pink, about 3 to 5 minutes per side.

Tuna Steaks

Serves 4

Ingredients

olive oil
2 teaspoons lime juice
1 fresh chilli, minced
3 cloves garlic, minced
salt and pepper, to taste
4 tuna steaks

Method

Whisk the olive oil, lime juice, chilli, garlic, salt and pepper together in a flat bottomed dish.

Place the tuna steaks in the dish, turning to coat entirely in marinade.

Refrigerate for 20 minutes.

Preheat barbecue for high heat and lightly oil the grate.

Cook the steaks until they are beginning to firm and are hot in the center, 5–6 minutes per side.

Grilled Salmon with Garlic Lemon Butter

Serves 6

Ingredients

120 g (4 oz) unsalted butter
4 cloves garlic, smashed
45 ml (1½ fl oz) fresh lemon juice, plus lemon wedges to serve
fresh dill, chopped, plus more to garnish
1 teaspoon salt
¼ teaspoon black pepper
1 kg salmon (approx. 2 lb) skin on, cut into 6 fillets

Method

Melt butter over medium heat. Smash 4 garlic cloves with the flat of a large knife and add to butter along with 1 teaspoon salt and ¼ teaspoon pepper.

Simmer 2 minutes or until fragrant. Add chopped dill and lemon juice then remove from heat.

Transfer half of sauce to a small bowl. Reserve and set aside remaining sauce in the pan – you will use this for serving. Arrange salmon fillets on a platter skin-side-down and brush tops with ¼ of the sauce from the bowl. Let salmon marinate in refrigerator 15 minutes while grill preheats.

Preheat grill to medium/high. Brush the hot grill clean and oil the grates.

Place salmon onto preheated grill, skin-side down.

Cover and grill over medium/high heat undisturbed, about 2 minutes on the first side.

Carefully flip salmon over, cover and cook another 2 minutes.

Flip again and (while wearing the oven mitt and starting with the fillets at the back), brush tops with ¼ of remaining sauce.

Cover and continue grilling just until salmon is flaky and cooked through (approx. another 1 minute).

Remove salmon from grill and drizzle with sauce reserved in saucepan.

Garnish with fresh dill and serve with lime wedges to squeeze over salmon if desired.

Salmon Fillets with Thai Dressing

Serves 4

Ingredients

4 skinless salmon fillets
350 g (12 oz) jasmine rice
60 g (2 oz) sesame seeds
45 ml (1½ fl oz) olive oil
240 ml (8 fl oz) Thai marinade
bunch of spring onions

Method

Steam the rice, mix through the sesame seeds and place in a container suitable for reheating.

Rub the salmon with oil and pour over the Thai marinade, making sure it covers both sides of the fish. Cover and set aside for 20 minutes.

Cut the spring onions diagonally into 2.5 cm (1 in) lengths, including some of the green tops. Place onto 2 foil squares, pour over a little of the marinade and wrap into a parcel with a double fold top and sides.

Take everything to the barbecue area.

Prepare the barbecue for direct-heat grilling and heat to hot.

Place the steamed rice at edge of the grill to keep hot. Oil the grill well.

Place the salmon and the foil parcel of spring onions on the grill and cook for 2 minutes. Turn the salmon and the foil parcel and cook for 2 minutes more. Remove the parcel. Cook the salmon until done. Divide the onions between 4 plates on top of a mound of rice and the Thai salmon. Serve immediately.

Thai Marinade

Serves 4

Ingredients

1 teaspoon sesame oil
1 teaspoon chilli oil
1 teaspoon peanut oil
1 onion, grated
2 teaspoons freshly minced garlic
2 teaspoons freshly minced ginger
2 red capsicums, roasted, deseeded, skin removed and finely diced
1 whole lime, juiced
2 teaspoons light soy sauce
4 teaspoons freshly ground black pepper
45 g (1½ oz) brown sugar
1 red chilli, cut lengthwise
360 ml (12 fl oz) water
1 teaspoon corn flour
1 small bunch coriander (cilantro) leaves, stalks removed, finely chopped

Method

Pour all the oils into a saucepan. Add the onion and fry for 2 minutes, stirring occasionally.

Add garlic and ginger and continue to fry for 2 more minutes.

Add all the other ingredients except the water, corn flour and coriander (cilantro).

Stir the ingredients thoroughly.

Add a little of the water to the corn flour and work into a paste.

Add the rest of the water to the corn flour, and then add the mixture to the pot. Stir to combine and simmer for 10 minutes.

Add coriander (cilantro) and cook for another 2 minutes.

Allow to cool.

Remove the 2 chilli pieces and transfer marinade to an airtight container.

Can be stored in the refrigerator for approximately 6–8 weeks.

Grilled Sardines

Serves 4–6

Ingredients

12 sardines, cleaned
¼ cup extra virgin olive oil
sea salt
1 lemon, cut into wedges
chopped parsley

Salad

1 green capsicum (bell pepper)
1 yellow capsicum (bell pepper)
3 tomatoes, diced
1 red onion, diced
2 tablespoons extra virgin olive oil
1 tablespoon white wine vinegar
½ teaspoon sugar
salt and freshly ground black pepper

Method

Place sardines in a large shallow ceramic dish.

Drizzle with olive oil and sprinkle over salt, cover with cling wrap and refrigerate for 1–2 hours.

Preheat a grill or barbecue. Cook sardines for 3–4 minutes each side or until golden and cooked.

To make salad, cut green and yellow capsicum in four and remove seeds.

Place on a baking tray under a hot grill for 6–8 minutes or until skin blisters.

Leave to cool, then remove skin and dice.

Toss together capsicum, tomatoes, onion, olive oil, vinegar, sugar, salt and pepper.

Serve sardines with lemon wedges and the salad.

Seafood Paella

Serves 4–6

Ingredients

1 tablespoon olive oil
2 onions, chopped
2 cloves garlic, crushed
1 tablespoon fresh thyme leaves
2 teaspoons finely grated lemon zest
4 ripe tomatoes, chopped
2½ cups short-grain rice
pinch of saffron threads, soaked in 2 cups water
5 cups chicken or fish stock
300 g (10½ oz) fresh or frozen peas
2 red capsicums, chopped
1 kg (2¼ lb) mussels, scrubbed and beards removed
500 g (18 oz) firm white fish fillets, chopped
300 g (10½ oz) peeled uncooked prawns/shrimp, tails left intact
200 g (7 oz) scallops
3 calamari tubes, sliced
1 tablespoon chopped fresh parsley

Method

Preheat a barbecue to a medium heat. Place a large paella or frying pan on the barbecue, add the oil and heat.

Add the onions, garlic, thyme leaves and lemon zest and cook for 3 minutes or until the onion is soft.

Add the tomatoes and cook, stirring, for 4 minutes.

Add the rice and cook, stirring, for 4 minutes longer or until the rice is translucent.

Stir in the saffron mixture and stock and bring to a simmer.

Simmer, stirring occasionally, for 30 minutes or until the rice has absorbed almost all the liquid.

Stir in the peas, capsicum, mussels and cook for 2 minutes.

Add the fish, prawns and scallops and cook, stirring, for 2–3 minutes.

Stir in the calamari, parsley and cook, stirring, for 1–2 minutes longer or until the seafood is cooked.

Butterflied Prawns/Shrimp with Garlic, Chilli and Parsley

Serves 4–6

Ingredients

1 kg (about 20) green prawns/shrimp, shelled and deveined, tails left intact
2 tablespoons olive oil
1 tablespoon lemon juice
2 cloves garlic, crushed
2 red chillies, deseeded and finely chopped
2 tablespoons chopped fresh parsley
oil for frying
½ cup plain flour
lemon wedges to garnish

Method

Cut the prawns/shrimp down the back and remove the vein.

Combine the oil, lemon juice, garlic, chillies and parsley in a bowl. Add the prawns, mix well, and leave to marinate for 2–3 hours.

Heat the oil on medium on the flat plate of the barbecue, coat the prawns with flour, and cook quickly in the oil for 2–3 minutes. Drain on absorbent paper.

Serve with lemon wedges.

Asian Sea Scallops

Serves 4–6

Ingredients

20 scallops, in the shell
spray vegetable oil
spring onions, finely chopped, to taste
20 ml (⅔ fl oz) thick soy sauce
1 teaspoon green ginger, finely chopped
1 teaspoon lemongrass, the white section only, finely chopped
20 ml (⅔ fl oz) lime juice
1 small green chilli, seeds removed, finely chopped
10 ml (⅓ fl oz) water

Method

Check each scallop to see that it is clean and grit free. Lift each scallop out of the shell and give the shell a film of oil with the spray, then return the scallop. Repeat for all the scallops and refrigerate until ready to cook.

Mix the remaining ingredients together and spoon a little over each scallop in the shell.

Lift the scallops and shells onto a medium–hot barbecue grill – only cook a few at a time as they cook quickly. Turn the scallops carefully if you can, otherwise lift the shell from grill and turn the scallop away from the heat.

Spoon over a little more sauce, cook for a little longer and serve when they are done to your liking.

Barbecued Lobster Tails

Serves 4

Ingredients

4 raw lobster tails
90 g (3 oz) softened butter
2 teaspoons freshly crushed garlic
1 teaspoon lemon pepper
fresh coriander (cilantro), finely chopped, to taste
1 lemon, cut into wedges
chilli sauce if desired

Method

With kitchen scissors, cut each side of the soft shell of the underside of the lobster tails and remove.

Run a metal skewer through the length of each tail to keep them flat while cooking.

Soften the butter and mix the garlic, lemon pepper and coriander (cilantro) together.

Spread a coating on the lobster meat.

Take all to the barbecue area. Prepare the barbecue for direct-heat cooking, heat to high. Oil the grill bars well.

Place the lobster tails cut side down and cook for minutes to sear the meat.

Turn over to shell side down and cook for 5–8 minutes until the shell turns red and the meat is white and firm, but not dry.

Brush the meat twice with butter at intervals.

While the lobsters are cooking place the lime wedges on the grill to color a little. Brush with chilli sauce if desired.

Remove the lobsters to a platter, place a teaspoon of butter on top, garnish with grilled lime wedges.

Grilled Lobster with Chilli Salsa

Serves 2–4

Ingredients

2 cooked lobsters, about 650 g (1 lb 6 oz) each
4 teaspoons olive oil
½ teaspoon Cayenne pepper

Chilli Salsa

2 tablespoons olive oil
1 red capsicum (bell pepper), deseeded and diced
1 small onion, chopped
1 large red chilli, deseeded and finely chopped
1 tablespoon sun-dried tomato purée
salt and freshly ground black pepper

Method

To make salsa, heat oil in a saucepan and fry red capsicum, onion and chilli for 5 minutes or until tender.

Stir in the tomato purée and season to taste. Transfer to a bowl.

To cut lobsters in half lengthwise, turn one on its back. Cut through the head end first, using a large, sharp knife, then turn lobster round and cut through the tail end. Discard the small greyish sac in the head – everything else in the shell is edible.

Crack the large claws with a small hammer or wooden rolling pin.

Repeat with the second lobster.

Drizzle the cut side of lobsters with oil and sprinkle with Cayenne pepper.

Heat grill on barbecue on medium heat and add lobster halves, and cook for 2–3 minutes until the lightly golden.

Serve with Chilli Salsa.

VEGETABLES

Balsamic Vegetables

Serves 4

Ingredients

2 large zucchini (courgette)
1 red capsicum (pepper)
1 yellow capsicum (pepper)
1 green capsicum (pepper)
3 beetroot
1 large eggplant (aubergine)
2 red onions
2 tablespoons balsamic vinegar
2 garlic cloves, crushed
2 tablespoons thyme
2 tablespoons basil
3 tablespoons olive oil
balsamic glaze

Method

Cut all of the vegetables to equal size.

Place on a lightly oiled, medium high grill until lightly browned and have a grill marked appearance.

Place in a foil barbecue roasting tray lined with baking paper.

Combine the balsamic vinegar, garlic, thyme, basil and oil in a bowl and whisk.

Add the dressing to the vegetables and toss to coat.

Place the tray on a medium–high barbecue grill and close the lid.

Roast, tossing every 5–10 minutes, until golden and tender.

Dress with the balsamic glaze and serve.

Grilled Asparagus

Serves 4

Ingredients

2 bunches asparagus
3 tablespoons olive oil
salt and pepper, to season
balsamic glaze

Method

Snap off the woody part of the asparagus, then toss in the olive oil.

Cook the asparagus on a medium–hot barbecue grill for 2–3 minutes, then turn over and cook for a further 2–3 minutes or until charred and tender.

Serve on a platter and drizzle with balsamic glaze just before serving.

Stuffed Jalapeño Chillies

Serves 4–6

Ingredients

12 jalapeño chillies
100 g (3½ oz) grated cheddar cheese
250 g (9 oz) cream cheese
50 g (1¾ oz) bacon, finely diced
12 small bacon strips, to wrap over the top of the chillies

Method

Cut the tops off the chillies and de-seed (an apple corer works quite well, gloves are a good idea also).

Combine the cheese and diced bacon.

Fill each jalapeño with the cheese mixture and place a strip of bacon over the top to seal using a toothpick.

Place upright on a chilli board and place over medium–high barbecue grill for 10–15 minutes, or cooked to your liking.

Sweet Potato Wedges

Serves 2–4

Ingredients

2 large sweet potatoes, scrubbed and cut into wedges
3 tablespoons olive oil

Seasoning mix

1 tablespoon coarse salt
1 tablespoon paprika
1 tablespoon chilli powder
1 tablespoon cracked black pepper

Method

Make the seasoning mix by combining the salt, paprika, chilli powder and cracked black pepper.

Placed the potato wedges in a large bowl, add the olive oil and toss until all of the wedges are coated in oil.

Sprinkle with the seasoning mix (reserve some of the seasoning to garnish at the end) and toss again until the wedges are well coated with seasoning.

Place the wedges on the barbecue grill on a medium heat for 30 minutes, turning every 5 minutes. When cooked a knife, will pass through the wedge easily.

Place the wedges on a serving platter and garnish with the remaining seasoning mix to serve.

Vegetable Skewers

Serves 2–4

Ingredients

8 wooden or bamboo skewers
2 zucchinis cut into 2½ cm (1 in) slices
2 yellow squash, cut into 2½ cm (1 in) slices
¼ kg (9 oz) whole fresh mushrooms
1 red onion, cut into chunks
12 cherry tomatoes
1 red bell pepper, cut into chunks
½ cup olive oil
1½ teaspoons dried basil
¾ teaspoon dried oregano
½ teaspoon salt
1 teaspoon ground black pepper

Method

Soak skewers in water for 30 minutes.

Preheat grill for medium heat and lightly oil the grate.

Alternately thread zucchini slices, yellow squash slices, mushrooms, onion, tomatoes and bell pepper onto the skewers.

Whisk olive oil, basil, oregano, salt, and black pepper in a bowl; brush mixture over vegetables.

Cook skewers on preheated grill until vegetables are tender, turning and basting vegetables with olive oil mixture occasionally, 10–15 minutes.

Garlic Grilled Beans

Serves 4–6

Ingredients

1 bag of fresh green beans, trimmed
¼ cup olive oil
1 teaspoon minced garlic
1 teaspoon kosher salt

Method

Combine green beans, olive oil, garlic, and salt in a bowl; toss to coat.

Allow green beans to marinate for 30 minutes.

Preheat grill for medium heat and lightly oil the grate.

Arrange green beans on a grill pan.

Place grill pan on preheated grill; cook and stir green beans until lightly charred, about 10 minutes.

Grilled Eggplant

Serves 2

Ingredients

large eggplant
½ cup butter or margarine, melted
½ teaspoon garlic salt
½ teaspoon Italian seasoning
½ teaspoon salt
¼ teaspoon pepper

Method

Peel the eggplant, and then cut into 2 cm slices.

Combine butter, garlic salt, and Italian seasonings; stir well.

Brush eggplant slices with butter mixture, and sprinkle with salt and pepper.

Place eggplant on grill; grill over medium heat 10 minutes or until tender, turning and basting occasionally.

Grilled Haloumi Cheese

Serves 2–4

Ingredients

½ tablespoon olive oil
170 g (6 oz) haloumi cheese, cut into 1 cm (¾ in) thick sticks
2 teaspoons fresh lemon juice
¼ teaspoon dried oregano
black pepper, to taste
sliced chilli

Method

Heat the grill to a medium–high heat. Add the haloumi sticks, and cook until the cheese turns light, golden-brown, 1–2 minutes on each side.

Sprinkle with lemon juice, oregano and pepper. Serve immediately alongside a salad or vegetables and garlic bread.

Garlic Smashed Potatoes

Serves 4

Ingredients

500 g (18 oz) potatoes
salt
4 tbsp. melted butter
6–8 cloves garlic
2tsp rosemary leaves roughly chopped
ground black pepper

Method

Preheat barbecue to 210 °C (410°F).

In a large pot, cover potatoes with water and add a generous pinch of salt.

Bring water to a boil and simmer until potatoes are tender, about 15 minutes.

Drain and let sit until cool enough to handle.

On a large rimmed baking sheet, toss potatoes with melted butter, garlic, and rosemary.

Using bottom of a glass, press down on potatoes to smash them into flat patties.

Season with salt and pepper cook until bottoms of potatoes are beginning to crisp around 25–30 minutes.

Corn on the Cob

Serves 4

Ingredients

4 corns on the cob
30 g (1 oz) butter, melted, plus extra to serve
salt and freshly ground black pepper, to taste

Method

Strip the silk off the corn.

Brush the corn with melted butter and sprinkle with salt and freshly ground black pepper.

Replace the husks and secure in three places with string.

Barbecue the corn cobs over hot grill for 15–20 minutes, or until tender, turning frequently.

When cooked, the husks will be dry and brown and the corn will be golden brown.

Serve with melted butter and salt and pepper.

Chilli Butter Corn Cobs

Serves 3–6

Ingredients

6 sweet corn cobs, in their husk
250 g (9 oz) butter, softened
2–3 jalapeños, finely diced
1 red onion, finely diced
½ bunch coriander, finely chopped
½ teaspoon pepper

Method

To prepare the corn, pull the silk off but leave the husk on (don't break off).

Soak the corn in a bowl of water for 30 minutes.

Preheat the grill to medium–high heat and grill the ears for 10 minutes. Pull the husk back and continue to grill on a lightly oil brushed grill, turning occasionally, until the kernels are tender and charred in spots (about 10 minutes).

Combine the butter, jalapeños, red onion, coriander and pepper. Place the butter in fridge if required.

Once cooked, lather the corn with the chilli butter and serve.

Hot Potato Cakes

Serves 4

Ingredients

800 g (1¾ lb) potatoes, peeled
1 tablespoon butter
¾ cup sour cream
1 teaspoon chopped chives
¼ cup plain flour
¾ teaspoon baking powder
dill, finely chopped, to serve
sour cream, to serve

Method

Boil the potatoes until tender, drain and mash. Stir in the butter, sour cream, chives, our and baking powder.

Form into patties using about ¼ cup of mash for each.

Place onto a tray, refrigerate until ready to cook.

Prepare barbecue for direct-heat cooking.

Heat the grill plate to hot and oil well.

Place the potato cakes on the grill, cook until brown on both sides. Keep warm.

Serve with a dipping bowel of sour cream and garnish with dill.

Caramelized Onions

Serves 2–4

Ingredients

1–2 tablespoons butter
3 large onions, halved and sliced
salt, to taste
1 tablespoon brown sugar
1–2 teaspoons balsamic vinegar

Method

Melt the butter in a frying pan over a low heat.

Add the onions and salt and cook slowly until the onions are soft and golden brown, stirring occasionally so they do not catch on the bottom of the pan.

Add the sugar and the vinegar.

Cook for a further 10 minutes stirring occasionally until sticky and brown.

Use immediately or allow to cool and store in a glass container, in the fridge.

Barbecue Potatoes

Serves 4

Ingredients

4–6 medium sized potatoes, washed
1 tablespoon oil
1 teaspoon salt
butter or sour cream as desired

Method

Place the washed potatoes in a bowl. Combine the oil and salt, pour over potatoes and toss to coat.

Wrap each potato in a piece of foil.

Place potatoes on the barbecue grill as soon as you light the barbecue. The potatoes will heat and get a head start before it is hot enough to cook.

Turn the potatoes at times.

When barbecue heats up, turn the potatoes more frequently.

Test with a skewer. If soft, remove and keep warm. Potatoes will take about 20 minutes with the slow start.

Fold the foil back from the potatoes. Cut a cross in the top and squeeze from the base to open out.

Squeeze a good dollop of cream or butter in the centre of potato and serve immediately.

Potato Wedges

Serves 2–4

Ingredients

4–6 medium-sized potatoes, peeled
1 teaspoon freshly crushed garlic
4 teaspoons finely chopped rosemary
2 fl oz (60 ml) olive oil
½ teaspoon lemon pepper
3 fl oz (90 ml) fresh lemon juice
salt, to taste

Method

Halve the potatoes then cut each half into 4–6 wedges. Place into a large bowl.

Mix the garlic, rosemary, oil and lemon juice together, pour over potatoes and toss well to coat.

Sprinkle with lemon pepper.

Cook over direct heat in a covered barbecue.

Cook for 20 minutes, turning the potatoes after 10 minutes.

Cook until tender and crisp.

The dish can be moved to indirect heat while other dishes finish cooking.

To serve, sprinkle lightly with salt.

SALADS

Sweet Coleslaw

Serves 2–4

Ingredients

1 small head cabbage, finely chopped
2 carrots, peeled and grated
1 red/Spanish onion, finely sliced

Dressing

1 cup whole egg mayonnaise
¼ cup apple cider
3 tablespoons sugar
salt and pepper, to taste

Method

In a large bowl, combine the cabbage, carrot and onion.

In a separate bowl; mix the mayonnaise, cider and sugar and season to taste.

Add the dressing to cabbage and coat well.

Refrigerate until required.

Potato Salad

Serves 4–6

Ingredients

1.5 kg (3 lb 5 oz) chat potatoes, whole and unpeeled
3 rashes bacon, rind and excess fat removed, then diced
¾ cup sour cream
½ cup whole egg mayonnaise
1 tablespoon wholegrain mustard
1 large red/Spanish onion, finely diced
1 bunch fresh chives, finely chopped
salt and pepper
hard boiled eggs (optional)

Method

Put the potatoes in a large saucepan, cover with water and add a teaspoon of salt. Place the saucepan over a medium heat and bring to the boil.

Reduce the heat and cook the potatoes until tender.

While the potatoes are cooking, cook the bacon on the barbecue, over a medium heat until crispy.

Remove from the heat and drain on some paper towels.

Once the potatoes are cooked, drain and set aside until cool to the touch.

Quarter the potatoes.

In a large bowl, mix together the sour cream, mayonnaise, wholegrain mustard and onion.

Add the potato and bacon and sprinkle with the fresh chives.

If you like, top the salad with a few halved boiled eggs.

Insalata Caprese

Serves 2–4

Ingredients

400 g (14 oz) Roma tomatoes, thickly sliced
250 g (9 oz) bocconcini/fresh mozzarella, sliced
½ cup fresh basil leaves, shredded
¼ cup extra-virgin olive oil
2 tablespoons balsamic vinegar
sea salt and freshly ground black pepper

Method

Arrange tomatoes, bocconcini, and basil leaves on individual plates.

Drizzle with olive oil and balsamic vinegar, and sprinkle with sea salt and freshly ground black pepper.

Serve with crusty bread.

Marinated Bean Salad

Serves 2–4

Ingredients

125 g (4½ oz) green beans, cut in half
2 small zucchini, cut into matchsticks
1 small carrot, cut into matchsticks
250 g (9 oz) canned red kidney beans,
drained and rinsed
250 g (9 oz) canned chickpeas, drained and rinsed
250 g (9 oz) canned lima beans, drained and rinsed
1 small red capsicum, cut into strips
¼ cup Italian parsley, chopped
¼ cup basil, chopped

Dressing

3 tablespoons extra-virgin olive oil
1½ tablespoons red wine vinegar
1 clove garlic, crushed
salt and freshly ground black pepper

Method

Steam the green beans, zucchini, and carrot until just tender.

Drain and rinse under cold running water.

To make dressing, place oil, vinegar, garlic, salt, and black pepper to taste in a screw-top jar and shake well to combine.

Place cooked vegetables, red kidney beans, chickpeas, lima beans, bell pepper, parsley, and basil in a large salad bowl.

Spoon dressing over salad and toss to combine.

Cover and refrigerate for 4–6 hours.

Just prior to serving, toss again.

Red Cabbage and Apple Slaw

Serves 2–4

Ingredients

1 small red cabbage, shredded
2 granny smith apples, julienned
½ small red onion, finely sliced
1 small bunch flat-leaf parsley

Dressing

3 tablespoons whole-egg mayonnaise
3 tablespoons sour cream
3 tablespoons cider vinegar
1 teaspoon Dijon mustard
1 tablespoon honey
salt and pepper, to taste

Method

Combine the cabbage, apple and onion in a large bowl.

In a separate bowl, mix together the mayonnaise, sour cream, vinegar, Dijon and honey and season to taste.

Add the dressing to the slaw and toss well. Garnish with parsley.

Refrigerate until needed.

Watercress and Pear Salad

Serves 2–4

Ingredients

2 bunches watercress, picked over and washed
shavings of Parmesan cheese
3 tablespoons extra-virgin olive oil
1 tablespoon lemon juice
½ tablespoon white wine vinegar
salt and freshly ground black pepper
3 bosc pears, finely sliced

Method

Wash and dry the watercress well.

Slice pears finely and combine with watercress in a bowl.

Whisk the olive oil, lemon juice, and white wine vinegar with salt and pepper until the mixture has thickened slightly.

Drizzle just enough dressing to coat the leaves.

Place on a platter and top with shavings of Parmesan.

Thai Beef Salad

Serves 2–4

Ingredients

500 g (18 oz) round steak
salt and freshly ground black pepper
1 small red chilli, finely chopped
45 ml (1½ fl oz) lime juice
45 ml (1½ fl oz) fish sauce
30 g (1 oz) brown sugar
1 teaspoon sesame oil
¼ Chinese cabbage, finely shredded
30 g (1 oz) coriander (cilantro) sprigs
30 g (1 oz) mint sprigs
120 g (4 oz) snow peas, trimmed
1 cucumber, sliced
1 small red onion, thinly sliced
210 g (7 oz) cherry tomatoes, halved

Method

Trim any excess fat and sinew from the steak. Season with salt and black pepper.

Cook the steak on a lightly oiled grill on the barbecue for a few minutes until medium rare.

Remove and rest for 10 minutes before slicing across the grain into thin strips.

Put the chilli, lime juice, fish sauce, brown sugar, and sesame oil in a small bowl and whisk to combine.

Combine the cabbage, half the cilantro, the mint, snow peas, cucumber, onion, and tomatoes on a large salad platter or on individual plates.

Top with the sliced steak, drizzle with dressing, and garnish with the remaining cilantro.

Caesar Salad

Serves 2

Ingredients

2 baby cos lettuce, broken
30 g (1 oz) croutons
4 bacon rashers, diced
100 g (3½ oz) shaved parmesan
4 boiled eggs

Dressing

2 tablespoons mayonnaise
1 garlic clove, crushed
1 teaspoon Worcestershire sauce
1 teaspoon Dijon mustard
3 tablespoons lemon juice
salt and pepper, to taste
125 ml (4½ fl oz) light olive oil
25 g (1 oz) finely grated Parmesan cheese

Method

To make the dressing, add all of the ingredients except the oil and cheese to a food processor.

Blend, adding the oil in a slow stream.

Continue until the dressing thickens, then stop and add the cheese and pulse until combined.

Break up the lettuce into small pieces and place into a serving bowl.

Add the croutons, bacon, Parmesan cheese and boiled eggs.

Top with the dressing just before serving.

Barbecued Seafood Salad

Serves 2–4

Ingredients

2 tablespoons lemon juice
1 tablespoon olive oil
300 g (¾ cup) firm white fleshed fish such as
swordfish, mackerel, or cod, cut into 25 mm (1 in) cubes
300 g (¾ cup) pink fleshed fish such as salmon, marlin, or tuna, cut into 25 mm (1 in) cubes
12 scallops
12 raw shrimp/prawns (peeled or unpeeled)
4 calamari tube, cut into rings
1 bunch watercress, broken into sprigs
1 large red onion, cut into rings
1 long cucumber, peeled and thinly sliced

Method

Place lemon juice and oil in a bowl. Whisk to combine. Add fish, scallops, shrimp, and calamari. Toss to combine. Cover and marinate in the refrigerator for 1 hour or until ready to use (do not marinate for longer than 2 hours).

For the dressing, place tarragon, vinegar, lemon juice, oil, salt, and black pepper in a screw-top jar. Shake to combine and set aside.

Preheat a barbecue or broiler until very hot. Line a serving platter with watercress.

Drain seafood mixture and place on barbecue plate or in broiler pan.

Add onion and cook, turning several times, for 6–8 minutes or until seafood is just cooked. Take care not to overcook or the seafood will be tough and dry.

Transfer seafood to a bowl.

Add cucumber and dressing of choice. Toss to combine.

Spoon seafood mixture over watercress and serve immediately.

Chicken & Avocado Salad

Serves 4

Ingredients

3 skinless chicken breasts, cooked and sliced
1 small head of romaine lettuce, shredded
1 large red onion, thinly sliced
½ cup extra-virgin olive oil
¼ cup red wine vinegar
salt and freshly ground black pepper
2 avocados, peeled and sliced

Method

Place chicken, lettuce, and onion in a bowl.

Thoroughly combine oil and vinegar, and season to taste with salt and pepper. Pour over salad, toss gently, then arrange chicken on a serving plate.

Garnish with avocado and serve.

Pearl Couscous Salad

Serves 2–4

Ingredients

170 g (6 oz) pearl couscous
400 g (14 oz) tinned four-bean mix
2 large tomatoes, deseeded and diced
1 cucumber, peeled, deseeded and diced
1 small red onion, diced
¼ teaspoon salt
½ teaspoon cracked black pepper
2 tablespoons olive oil
3 tablespoons balsamic vinegar

Method

Heat 250 ml (1 cup) of water in a saucepan over high heat until just at a high simmer.

Add the pearl couscous and cover, simmering, for about 10 minutes.

Stir every couple of minutes.

The grains will fluff up just slightly and should be al dente when cooked.

Set aside to cool.

Drain and rinse the four-bean mix. Place the bean mix in a large bowl along with the pearl couscous, tomato, cucumber and red onion. Season with salt and the cracked black pepper.

Add the olive oil and balsamic vinegar and mix until all of the ingredients are combined.

Place in the fridge until ready to serve.

Tomato & Onion with Feta Dressing

Serves 2–4

Ingredients

4 large tomatoes, thinly sliced
1 red onion, thinly sliced
salt and freshly ground black pepper
¼ cup fresh basil, chopped

Dressing

75 g (2½ oz) feta, crumbled
3 tablespoons plain yogurt
2 tablespoons extra-virgin olive oil
1 tablespoon white wine vinegar

Method

Arrange the tomato and onion slices on a large serving plate and season with salt and pepper.

In a food processor or using a hand mixer, blend the feta, yogurt, oil, and vinegar until smooth.

Drizzle the dressing over the tomatoes, then sprinkle with basil.

Tomato & Mozzarella Salad

Serves 2–4

Ingredients

6 Roma tomatoes, sliced
250 g (9 oz) buffalo mozzarella, drained and sliced
2 scallions/shallots, sliced
90 g (3 oz) black olives
salt and freshly ground black pepper

Dressing

3 tablespoons extra-virgin olive oil
1 clove garlic, crushed
2 teaspoons balsamic vinegar
¼ cup fresh basil, chopped

Method

Arrange the tomatoes, mozzarella, scallions, and olives in layers on serving plates and season.

To make the dressing, heat the oil and garlic in a small saucepan over a very low heat for 2 minutes or until the garlic has softened but not browned.

Remove the pan from the heat, add the vinegar and basil, then pour it over the salad.

Greek Salad

Serves 2

Ingredients

2 English cucumbers, sliced
4 Roma tomatoes, quartered
2 red onions, quartered
85 g (3 oz) feta, crumbled
½ cup Kalamata olives, left whole
3 tablespoons extra-virgin olive oil
2 tablespoons red wine vinegar
pinch of sea salt
freshly ground black pepper, to taste
2 tablespoons or ¼ cup oregano leaves

Method

Place the cucumber, tomatoes, onion, feta, and olives in a bowl.

Whisk together the olive oil and vinegar in a separate bowl.

Pour the dressing over the salad, then season with salt and pepper.

Garnish with oregano leaves.

Serve the salad on its own or with fresh bread.

Waldorf Salad

Serves 2

Ingredients

1 green apple
1 red apple
juice of ½ lemon
1 cup celery, finely chopped
½ cup walnuts, chopped
60 g (2 oz) mayonnaise
crisp lettuce cups
1 red apple, thinly sliced, brushed with lemon juice to prevent discoloration, to garnish

Method

Chill apples, then core and dice them.

Pour lemon juice over apples.

Add celery, walnuts and mayonnaise and combine.

Serve piled into lettuce cups and garnish with slices of red apple.

Crab Salad

Serves 2

Ingredients

400 g (14 oz) crabmeat, fresh or canned
4 crisp celery sticks, finely chopped
125 ml (4 fl oz) French dressing
salt and freshly ground black pepper, to taste
4 small butter lettuces, shredded
4 sprigs chives, to garnish

Method

In a mixing bowl, combine crabmeat and celery.

Moisten with French dressing and salt and pepper and mix well.

Line a salad bowl with the shredded lettuce.

Pile the crab on top.

Add some more dressing, scatter with chives just before serving.

Potato Salad with Bacon and Boiled Eggs

Serves 4

Ingredients

1.5 kg (3 lb 5 oz) chat potatoes, whole and unpeeled
3 bacon rashers, rind and excess fat removed and diced
185 g (6½ fl oz) sour cream
125 g (4½ fl oz) whole-egg mayonnaise
1 tablespoon wholegrain mustard
1 small red onion, finely diced
1 bunch chives, finely chopped
salt and pepper, to season
4 hard-boiled eggs

Method

Put the potatoes in a large saucepan, cover with water and pinch of salt.

Place the saucepan over medium heat and bring to the boil.

Reduce the heat and cook the potatoes until tender.

Once the potatoes are cooked, drain and let them steam dry.

Once cool to the touch, quarter.

Meanwhile, cook the bacon in a frying pan over medium heat until crispy.

Remove the bacon from the pan and drain on paper towel.

In a small bowl, mix together the sour cream, mayonnaise, wholegrain mustard and onion.

In a serving bowl, add the potato and combine with the sour cream and mayo mixture.

Sprinkle with the bacon and chives. Top with the boiled eggs.

Warm Thai Chicken Salad

Serves 4–6

Ingredients

3 chicken breasts
2 teaspoons Thai seasoning
1 teaspoon oil
1 red bell pepper/capsicum, seeded and cut into strips
1 green bell pepper/capsicum, seeded and cut into strips
1 eggplant, sliced
1 red onion, cut into rings
½ head of romaine lettuce, shredded

Dressing

½ cup extra-virgin olive oil
1¼ cups malt vinegar
1 teaspoon Thai seasoning

Method

Pound the chicken breasts slightly until they reach an even thickness.

Mix the Thai seasoning and oil together and rub well into the chicken.

Cover and let stand for 20 minutes before cooking.

Heat the grill to medium–high and oil the hotplate or the grill bars.

Place the chicken on the grill and cook for 4 minutes on each side.

Place the vegetables (except the lettuce) on the hotplate, drizzle with a little oil, and cook for 5–8 minutes, tossing and turning to cook through.

Pile lettuce onto individual plates and place the barbecued vegetables in the center.

Cut the chicken into thin diagonal slices and arrange over and around the vegetables.

Mix the dressing ingredients together and pour over the salad.

Serve with crusty bread.

Lamb Backstrap with Sweet Potato Chopped Salad

Serves 4–8

Ingredients

3 lamb backstraps
400 g (14 oz) rocket leaves and mixed leaves
2 sweet potatoes, cut into 1 cm cubes (to be roasted)
2–3 small beetroot, cooked and cubed
1 small red onion, finely sliced
75 g (3 oz) crumbled feta
3 bacon rashers, cooked and diced
50 g (1¾ oz) pine nuts, roasted
100 g (3½ oz) roasted red capsicum (pepper), sliced into strips

Barbecue rub

50 ml (2 fl oz) olive oil
salt and pepper, to taste
honey lemon mustard dressing
spiced avocado yogurt dressing

Method

Rub the lamb back straps with oil and barbecue rub let marinate for 30 minutes then on a hot grill cook for 3–4 minutes each side then rest for10 minutes.

Prepare both the dressings and put them in the fridge until required.

Peel and cube the sweet potato place in a large bowl then microwave for 4–5 minutes until tender, dress with an enough oil to coat the potato and season with salt and pepper.

Then place in a shallow oven tray on a medium hot barbecue with the hood down for 10–15 minutes or until browned once done set aside.

On a medium hot barbecue cook off the bacon to your liking and set aside to dress the salad later.

Slice the lamb back strap into thin slices then on serving platter add the leaves, onion and toss, then top with the lamb slices, sweet potato cubes, beetroot, feta, capsicum and bacon.

When ready to serve top with both the honey lemon mustard and spiced avocado yogurt dressing and pine nuts.

Baby Octopus Salad

Serves 4–6

Ingredients

12 baby octopuses
2 teaspoons coriander seeds, toasted
2 cloves garlic, finely minced, plus 12 cloves, sliced
2 tablespoons lemon juice
¼ cup sweet chilli sauce
2 cucumbers, peeled
1 large red bell pepper/capsicum
1 bunch watercress
1 cup pickled ginger
1 tablespoon black sesame seeds
1 cup cilantro/coriander leaves
1 cup bean sprouts
1 cup canola oil
pinch of sea salt

Method

Clean octopuses by peeling off skin and removing heads.

Grind toasted coriander seeds in a mortar and pestle. Combine coriander, minced garlic, lemon juice, and sweet chilli sauce in bowl. Add octopus and marinate in refrigerator for 2 hours.

Using a vegetable peeler, peel thin strips of cucumber. Thinly slice bell pepper lengthwise. Combine watercress, cucumber, bell pepper, pickled ginger, sesame seeds, cilantro leaves and bean sprouts in a large bowl. Set aside.

Heat oil in a heavy-based skillet and fry sliced garlic until golden brown and crispy. Remove and drain on a paper towel.

Strain marinade from the octopus into a small saucepan and bring to simmer. Set aside to cool and use as dressing later.

Heat a wok and stir-fry octopus until cooked, approximately 3–4 minutes. Combine prepared salad with octopus and toss with dressing. Season to taste.

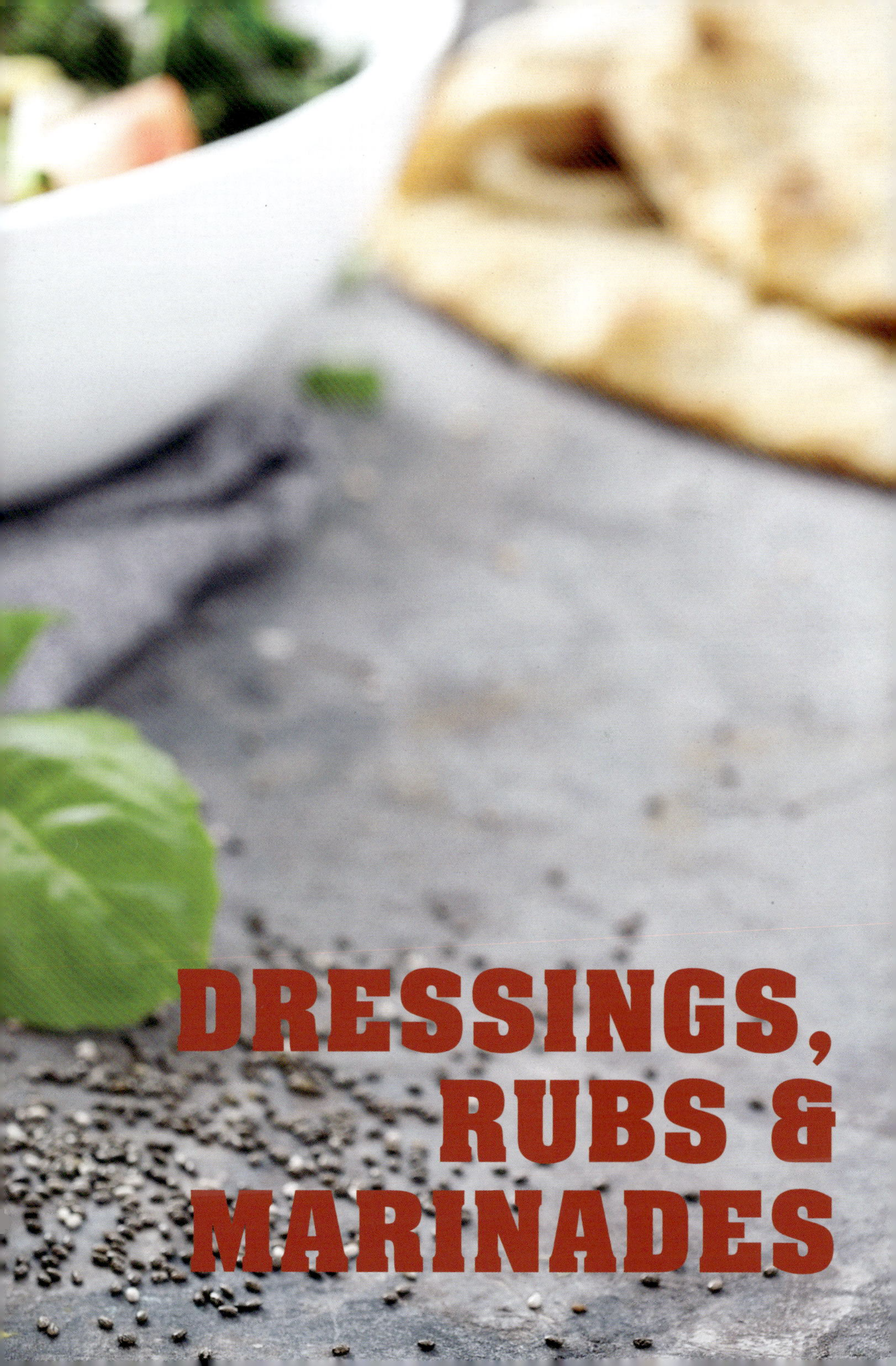

DRESSINGS, RUBS & MARINADES

Blue Cheese

Serves 2 cups

Ingredients

¼ teaspoon dry mustard
2 egg yolks
1 cup extra-virgin olive oil
2 tablespoons lemon juice or white wine vinegar
salt and freshly ground black pepper
90 g (3 oz) blue cheese, crumbled

Method

Place mustard and egg yolks in a food processor or blender and process until just combined.

With machine running, gradually pour in oil and process until mixture thickens. Blend in lemon juice or vinegar and season to taste.

Add the blue cheese and process to combine.

Real Homemade Herb Mayonnaise

Serves 2–3

Ingredients

1¼ cups olive oil
1¼ cups grapeseed oil
2 cups fresh herbs of your choice, such as Italian parsley, chives, basil, chervil
2 cloves garlic, peeled
2 eggs, plus 2 yolks
1 tablespoon Dijon mustard
1 tablespoon white wine vinegar
salt and freshly ground black pepper

Method

Combine the olive and grapeseed oils and set aside. Process the herbs and garlic until chopped and set aside.

Place the eggs and yolks in a food processor and process for 2 minutes.

With machine running, add the mustard and half the vinegar, and then add the oil mixture in a thin stream.

When most of the oil has been used, stop the processor and add the herb mixture, remaining vinegar and oil, and process briefly to combine.

Add salt and pepper to taste and chill until ready to use.

Store in the refrigerator. Goes with everything.

Basic Vinaigrette

Serves 1

Ingredients

¾ cup extra-virgin olive oil
¼ cup cider vinegar
1 tablespoon Dijon mustard
salt and freshly ground black pepper

Method

Place oil, vinegar, mustard, salt and black pepper to taste in a screw-top jar and shake well to combine.

The foundation of many great salads where the freshness of the ingredients only needs simple embellishment.

Yogurt dressing

2 tablespoons snipped fresh chives
1 clove garlic, crushed
¾ cup natural yogurt
2 tablespoons white wine vinegar
salt and freshly ground black pepper

Method

Place chives, garlic, yogurt and vinegar in a bowl and whisk to combine.
Very versatile and a great vegetarian favourite.

Thousand Island Yogurt Dressing

Serves 1

Ingredients

2 tablespoons snipped fresh chives
¾ cup plain yogurt
2 tablespoons white wine vinegar
2 tablespoons green olives, chopped
2 scallions/shallots, finely chopped
1 hard-boiled egg, chopped
1 tablespoon finely chopped green bell pepper/capsicum
1 tablespoon tomato paste
½ teaspoon chilli sauce
pinch of salt

Method

Place all ingredients into a bowl and whisk to combine. Season to taste.

Store dressing in a screw-top jar in the refrigerator for up to 1 week.

Curried Yogurt Dressing

Serves 1

Ingredients

2 tablespoons snipped fresh chives
1 clove garlic, crushed
¾ cup plain yogurt
2 tablespoons white wine vinegar
1 teaspoon curry powder
dash of chilli sauce
pinch of sea salt

Method

Place chives, garlic, yogurt, vinegar, curry powder, and chilli sauce in a bowl and whisk to combine.

Season to taste.

Ginger & Soy Dressing

Serves 1 cup

Ingredients

5 cm (2 in) fresh ginger, minced
1 clove garlic, crushed
½ cup soy sauce
1 tablespoon cider vinegar
1 tablespoon sesame oil

Method

Place ginger, garlic, soy sauce, ½ cup water, the vinegar and oil in a screw-top jar and shake well to combine. Let stand for at least 15 minutes before using.

Store dressing in the jar in which you made it, in the refrigerator for 2–3 weeks.

Shake well and bring to room temperature before using.

Salad Dressing

Serves 1 cup

Ingredients

1 lemon juice
2 tablespoons Dijon mustard
250 ml (8 fl oz) olive oil
1 teaspoon salt
80 ml (2⅔ fl oz) balsamic vinegar
1 clove garlic, crushed
1 teaspoon fresh basil, finely chopped

Method

In a bowl, mix all ingredients well until combined.

Spiced Avocado Yogurt Dressing

Serves 1 cup

Ingredients

juice of ½ a lemon
½ avocado
2 tablespoons chopped flat-leaf parsley
½ teaspoon coriander powder
salt and pepper, to taste
125 g (4 fl oz) Greek-style yoghurt

Method

In a blender, add all ingredients except for the yoghurt.

Blend until smooth, then add the yoghurt. Stir to combine.

Refrigerate until needed.

Seafood Dressing

Serves 1 cup

Ingredients

125 ml (4 fl oz) tomato sauce
125 g (4 fl oz) mayonnaise
125 ml (4 fl oz) fresh cream

Method

Mix all ingredients together and chill before serving.

Dressing will keep well in the refrigerator for 5–7 days.

Honey Lemon Mustard Dressing

Serves 1 cup

Ingredients

juice of ½ a lemon
2 tablespoons honey
3 tablespoons olive oil
2 tablespoons Dijon mustard
salt and pepper, to taste

Method

Add all of the ingredients to a small jar and shake to combine.

Note: Store for up to 7 days in an airtight container in the fridge.

Garlic Mayonnaise

Serves 1 cup

Ingredients

¾ cup whole egg mayonnaise
2 tablespoons Greek yoghurt
1 teaspoon lemon juice
1 tablespoon parsley, finely chopped
1 garlic clove, minced

Method

Whisk the ingredients together in a small bowl.

Cover with cling wrap then refrigerate until ready to use.

Use within 7 days after preparation.

Béarnaise Sauce

Serves 1–2

Ingredients

1 shallot (scallion), chopped
½–1 tablespoons tarragon, chopped
sprig thyme
1 bay leaf
2 tablespoons tarragon vinegar
2 egg yolks
pinch of cayenne pepper
salt and freshly ground black pepper, to taste
1–2 tablespoons lemon juice or white wine vinegar
90 g (3 oz) butter

Method

In a small saucepan, infuse shallot, a little tarragon, thyme and bay leaf in vinegar for 2 minutes.

Bring this mixture to the boil, then simmer for 2–3 minutes. Strain.

Using a double boiler (or a bowl over a saucepan), place the egg yolks, seasonings and lemon juice into the top of the pan.

Whisk over hot water until the sauce begins to thicken.

Add the butter, in very small pieces, whisking in each piece until completely melted before adding the next – do not allow to boil, or it will curdle.

If the sauce is too thick, add a little cream.

Tartare Sauce

Serves 1–2 cups

Ingredients

1 cup mayonnaise (whole egg or Kewpie)
2 tablespoons gherkins, finely chopped
2 tablespoons chives, finely chopped
2 tablespoons fresh parsley, finely chopped
1 tablespoon Dijon mustard
juice of half a lemon
salt and pepper to taste

Method

In a small bowl, combine all ingredients.

Refrigerate until ready for use.

Tomato and Chilli Jam

Serves 1–2 cups

Ingredients

45 ml (1½ fl oz) olive oil
1 red/Spanish onion, finely chopped
2 cloves garlic, finely chopped
1 large red chilli, finely chopped
400 g (13 ½ oz) chopped tomatoes
10 sun-dried tomatoes, finely chopped
90 g (3 oz) brown sugar
45 ml (1½ oz) balsamic vinegar
salt and freshly ground black pepper

Method

Heat the olive oil in a pan, add the onion, garlic and chilli and cook for about five minutes, until onions softened.

Tip in the chopped tomatoes and sun-dried tomatoes and cook over a medium heat for about 10 minutes.

Add the sugar and vinegar and bring to a boil, stirring every now and then.

Balsamic Glaze

Serves 1–2 cups

Ingredients

125 ml (4½ fl oz) balsamic vinegar
50 ml (2 fl oz) tomato sauce
4 tablespoons barbecue sauce
½ cup brown sugar
1 garlic clove, crushed
1 tablespoon mustard
½ tablespoon cracked black pepper

Method

Combine the ingredients in a saucepan and bring to boil then reduce to a low heat until it has reduced by half and is a thick consistency.

Note: Store in an airtight container in the fridge.

Use as a glaze for asparagus, chicken or salmon when grilling.

Quick Tomato Salsa

Serves 2 cups

Ingredients

4–5 ripe tomatoes, de-seeded and diced
1 red/Spanish onion, finely diced
¼ cup fresh cilantro/coriander (or use 4 cup parsley)
1 teaspoon dried oregano
juice of half a lemon
1 tablespoon olive oil
salt and pepper to taste

Method

In a large bowl, toss together the diced tomatoes, onions, cilantro and oregano.

Squeeze the lemon juice over the tomato mix and drizzle with olive oil.

Season to taste, toss well and let everything marinate for 10–15 minutes.

Cover and refrigerate until serving.

Tomato and Chilli Jam Salsa

Serves 1–2

Ingredients

2 tablespoons olive oil
1 red/Spanish onion, finely chopped
2 cloves garlic, finely chopped
1 large red chilli, finely chopped
400 g (14 oz) chopped tomatoes
10 sun-dried tomatoes, finely chopped
½ cup brown sugar
2 tablespoons balsamic vinegar
salt and freshly ground black pepper

Method

Heat the olive oil in a pan, add the onion, garlic and chilli and cook for about five minutes, until onions softened.

Tip in the chopped tomatoes and sun-dried tomatoes and cook over a medium heat for about 10 minutes.

Add the sugar and vinegar and bring to a boil, stirring every now and then.

Reduce the heat. While the mixture is reducing, season to taste.

The jam is ready when it looks thick.

Sweet Plum Marinade

Makes 2 cups

Ingredients

1 ¼ cups plum conserve
¼ cup sugar
1 small red chilli, finely chopped
2 whole star anise
1 tablespoon Worcestershire sauce
1 teaspoon salt
juice of 1 medium lemon
¾ cup water
2 teaspoons cornflour

Method

Put the plum conserve into a skillet. Add all other ingredients except ¼ cup of water and the cornflour.

Stir to combine and simmer for 5 minutes.

Add a little of the water to the cornflour and work to a paste.

Add the rest of the water to the cornflour and then add to the plum marinade.

Stir to combine and simmer for another 5 minutes.

Allow to cool. Remove the star anise and transfer the marinade to an airtight container.

Makes approximately 2 cups in finished volume.

Can be stored in the refrigerator for approximately 6 weeks.

Thai Marinade

Makes 2½ cups

Ingredients

1 teaspoon sesame oil
1 teaspoon chilli oil
1 teaspoon peanut oil
1 onion, grated
2 teaspoons freshly minced garlic
2 teaspoons freshly minced ginger
2 red capsicums, roasted, deseeded, skin removed and finely diced
1 whole lime, juiced
2 teaspoons light soy sauce
1 tablespoon freshly ground black pepper
4 tablespoons brown sugar
1 red chilli, cut lengthwise
1½ cups water
1 teaspoon cornflour
1 small bunch coriander leaves, stalks removed, finely chopped

Method

Pour all the oils into a saucepan. Add the onion and fry for 2 minutes, stirring occasionally.

Add garlic and ginger and continue to fry for 2 more minutes.

Add all the other ingredients except the water, cornflour and coriander.

Stir the ingredients thoroughly.

Add a little of the water to the cornflour and work into a paste. Add the rest of the water to the cornflour, and then add the mixture to the pot. Stir to combine and simmer for 10 minutes.

Add coriander and cook for another 2 minutes.

Allow to cool. Remove the 2 chilli pieces and transfer marinade to an airtight container.

Can be stored in the refrigerator for approximately 6–8 weeks.

Satay Marinade

Serves 2 cups

Ingredients

½ teaspoon ground ginger
½ teaspoon ground coriander
¼ teaspoon ground cumin
½ onion, grated
2 tablespoons peanut oil
1 teaspoon freshly crushed garlic
¾ cup roasted peanuts, puréed into a paste
2 teaspoons tomato paste
¾ cup creamed coconut
3 tablespoons honey
¼ teaspoon salt

Method

Tip all the spices into a dry skillet and fry gently, stirring constantly until they begin to smoke.

Remove from the heat and continue to stir for another minute.

Add the grated onion and quickly combine.

Return to the heat and add the peanut oil.

Gently fry the spices and onion for 3–4 minutes, then add the garlic.

Fry for 1 minute, then add all other ingredients.

Simmer for 10 minutes.

Allow to cool, then transfer to an airtight container.

Makes approximately 2 cups in finished volume.

Can be stored in the refrigerator for approximately 1 week.

Barbecue Rub

Serves 1–2 cups

Ingredients

55 g (1¾ oz) brown sugar
2 teaspoons paprika
1 teaspoon salt
1 teaspoon mustard powder
1 teaspoon black pepper
1 teaspoon chilli flakes
1 teaspoon onion powder
1 teaspoon garlic powder

Method

Combine all of the ingredients.

Notes: Store in an airtight container for up to 6 months.

Increase the pepper and the mustard to make it hot and spicy by adding a few more teaspoons.

Smoky Barbecue Marinade

Serves 1 cup

Ingredients

1 tablespoon smoked paprika
2 tablespoons brown sugar
2 garlic cloves, finely chopped
¼ cup golden syrup
1 tablespoon white wine vinegar
1 tablespoon olive oil
2 tablespoon barbecue sauce

Method

In a mixing bowl, combine paprika, brown sugar, garlic, golden syrup, white wine vinegar, olive oil and barbecue sauce and mix well.

Rum and Barbecue Sauce

Serves 2 cups

Ingredients

1 teaspoon olive oil
1 small onion, finely grated
2 garlic cloves, crushed
250 ml (9 oz) tomato sauce
1 tablespoon soy sauce
1 teaspoon mustard powder
55 g (1¾ oz) brown sugar
125 ml (4½ fl oz) spiced rum

Method

Add the oil, onion and garlic to a small saucepan over medium heat and cook until the onion is transparent.

Add all the remaining ingredients, except the rum, and bring to the boil. Simmer for 20 minutes.

Remove from the heat, then add the rum and stir. Allow to cool.

Note: Store in an airtight container in the fridge for 1–2 weeks.

Rosemary and Garlic Seasoning

Serves 1 cup

Ingredients

1 teaspoon dried rosemary
2 teaspoons garlic powder
2 teaspoons onion powder
1 teaspoon black peppercorns
1 teaspoon salt

Method

Using a spice or coffee grinder, grind the rosemary and peppercorn into a powder.

In a small bowl, combine all of the ingredients. Note: Store in an airtight container for up to 6 months.

Cajun Seasoning

Serves 1 cup

Ingredients

2 teaspoons paprika
1 teaspoon salt
1 teaspoon black pepper
2 teaspoons garlic powder
2 teaspoons onion powder
1½ teaspoons dried thyme
1½ teaspoons dried basil
1 teaspoon cayenne pepper
1 teaspoon chilli flakes (optional)

Method

Combine all of the ingredients. Add the chilli flakes if you like.
Note: Store in an airtight container for up to 6 months.

Red Wine and Garlic Marinade

Makes 2 cups

Ingredients

1½ cups dry red wine
1 tablespoon fresh thyme, chopped
1 teaspoon salt
1 teaspoon freshly ground black pepper
3 tablespoons Worcestershire sauce
2 cloves garlic, finely chopped
3 tablespoons soy sauce
¾ cup water
3 teaspoons cornflour

Method

Put the red wine into a saucepan.

Add all other ingredients except ¼ cup of water and cornflour.

Stir to combine and simmer for 10 minutes.

Add a little of the water to the cornflour to make a paste.

Add the rest of the water to the cornflour, and then add to the marinade.

Stir to combine, and then simmer for a further 5 minutes. Adjust the seasoning.

Allow to cool and transfer to an airtight container.

Makes approximately 2 cups in finished volume.

Can be stored in the refrigerator for approximately 4 weeks.

PIZZA

Grilled Beer Dough Garlic Cheese Pizza

Serves 4

Ingredients

1 can of beer (whatever you are drinking will be fine)
2 teaspoons dry yeast
315 g (12½ oz) bread flour, plus 3 tablespoons extra, for rolling
1 teaspoon sugar
1 teaspoon salt
2 tablespoons olive oil
Parmesan, garlic and parsley butter
3 tablespoons grated cheese

Method

In a bowl, pour in the warm beer and add the yeast. Let it stand for about 10 minutes to activate the yeast. In another bowl, add the flour, sugar and salt. Slowly add the beer mixture to form a dry dough. Add a little more flour or beer if needed. Knead to form a nice elastic dough ball.

Place the ball into a large bowl that has been coated in the oil and rub some over the ball as well.

Cover with a tea towel and then let the dough rise for about 1 hour, or until roughly double its original size.

Knock down the dough and divide into 4 pieces depending on how big you want your pizzas. Roll intoballs and cover with a tea towel and rest for a further 10–15 minutes.

Take a ball and roll out. The shape doesn't matter as it doesn't need to be round. Brush a thin coat of olive oil on one side. Place the dough on a hot barbecue grill, oiled side down, and leave for about 3 minutes.

Using tongs, lift the edge to see if it has nice grill marks. Then flip it over to grill the other side.

Brush with melted parmesan, garlic and parsley butter and extra cheese. Close the lid on the barbecue (or take inside and put in a hot oven if you don't have a lid). When the cheese is melted to your liking, it's done.

Cut into slices and serve while warm.

Prosciutto Pizza

Serves 2–4

Ingredients

1 ball pizza doubt
¼ cup of pizza sauce
6–10 slices prosciutto
1 capsicum (bell pepper), sliced
450 g (2 cups) bocconcini cheese, sliced
10 fresh basil leaves, torn

Method

Set temperature to 230°C (445°F) and preheat, lid closed for 15 minutes.

Place a pizza stone directly on the grate while the grill preheats.

Heat the oil on a medium–hot barbecue flatplate.

Shape dough into a flat circle, pushing gently until fairly thin then transfer to a pizza tray.

Spread the sauce almost to the edges and arrange the prosciutto and sliced capsicum around the pizza, then top with sliced Bocconcini cheese.

Place Pizza Stone and bake for 12–15 minutes or until the crust is puffy and crisp.

Remove from barbecue and slice and serve hot.

Grilled Beer Dough Pizza with Spicy Italian Sausage & Sweet Peppers

Serves 4

Ingredients

1 tablespoon olive oil
4 spicy Italian sausages
2 large red onions, sliced
2 large red capsicums (peppers), halved and cut into 1 cm slices
125 g (4½ oz) grated gouda cheese

Method

Heat the oil on a medium–hot barbecue flatplate.

Squeeze out the sausage meat from their skins into roughly 2 cm (1 in) chunks.

Cook until charred and cooked through.

Meanwhile, add the onion and capsicum to the barbecue and cook until soft.

To prepare the pizza dough see recipe provided in this book.

Lemon Garlic Herb Butter

Serves 1 cup

Ingredients

100 g (3½ oz) softened butter
finely grated zest of 1 lemon, plus 1 teaspoon of juice
1 tablespoon finely chopped shallot
1 tablespoon finely chopped
flat-leaf parsley
1 garlic clove, crushed
salt and pepper, to taste

Method

Mix the ingredients in a bowl until smooth.

Place the mixture onto a piece of plastic wrap and roll into a tube shape, twisting the ends and tie.

Place in the freezer until firm, then cut into slices just before use.

Great spread over a fresh baguette and heated under the grill for easy garlic bread.

Bruschetta

Serves 2–4

Ingredients

8 Roma or plum tomatoes, finely chopped
1 medium red onion, finely chopped
10 basil leaves, chopped
salt, to taste
20 ml (⅔ fl oz) olive oil
30 ml (1 fl oz) balsamic dressing
1 baguette
1 large clove garlic, slightly crushed
105 g (3 ½ oz) butter
120 g (4 oz) fresh goats cheese

Method

In a bowl, combine the tomatoes, onion, basil leaves, salt, oil and balsamic dressing.

Cut the baguette into diagonal slices, rub with the raw garlic and spread with the butter.

Place on a hot barbecue grill and cook until golden brown.

Serve the fresh salsa and goats cheese on the hot garlic bread.

This salsa is good if prepared a few hours in advance.

Index

First published in 2022 by New Holland Publishers
Published in 2024 by New Holland Publishers
Sydney

Level 1, 178 Fox Valley Road, Wahroonga, NSW 2076, Australia

newhollandpublishers.com

A record of this book is held at the National Library of Australia.

ISBN 9781760796761

Managing Director: Fiona Schultz
Designer: Andrew Davies
Production Director: Arlene Gippert
Printed in China

10 9 8 7 6 5 4 3 2 1

Keep up with New Holland Publishers:
NewHollandPublishers
@newhollandpublishers